Emmanuel's
Book II

*Where the intellect
spins in frantic pursuit
of its own tail,
you know
you have found illusion—fear.*

Emmanuel's Book II

The Choice for Love

Compiled by
**Pat Rodegast and
Judith Stanton**

Illustrated by
Roland Rodegast

Introduction by
Ram Dass

BANTAM BOOKS
NEW YORK · TORONTO · LONDON · SYDNEY · AUCKLAND

EMMANUEL'S BOOK II:
The Choice for Love

A Bantam Book / October 1989

*Bantam New Age and the accompanying figure design as well as the statement
"the search for meaning, growth and change" are trademarks of Bantam Books,
a division of Bantam Doubleday Dell Publishing Group, Inc.*

Library of Congress Cataloging-in-Publication Data

Rodegast, Pat.
    Emmanuel's book II : the choice for love / Pat Rodegast and Judith Stanton.
      p.   cm.
    ISBN 0-553-34750-0
    1. Spirit writings.   2. Emmanuel (Spirit)   I. Stanton, Judith.   II. Title.
III. Title: Emmanuel's book 2.   IV. Title: Emmanuel's book two.
BF1301.R69   1989
133.9'3—dc19   89-131
                                                  CIP

Published simultaneously in the United States and Canada

---

*Bantam Books are published by Bantam Books, a division of Bantam Doubleday
Dell Publishing Group, Inc. Its trademark, consisting of the words "Bantam
Books" and the portrayal of a rooster, is Registered in U.S. Patent and Trademark
Office and in other countries. Marca Registrada, Bantam Books, 666 Fifth Ave-
nue, New York, New York 10103.*

To all who helped
in the preparation of this book:

You have brought to the human world
the words of spirit.

Through the work you allow us to do,
you build a golden bridge
between the world of illusion
and the world of perfect love.
For that,
both worlds thank you.

Emmanuel

Contents

Introduction: Uncle Emmanuel

When I was a child I had a wonderful uncle who brought me "surprises." Now, fifty years later, the spiritual child within me that is just waking up still delights in the thought of having a benevolent uncle who would give me gifts. But now, rather than material benefits, I would prefer that my special uncle share certain qualities with me.

The uncle I might look for now would be wise and compassionate, with a dry sense of humor; tough yet tender; someone who would keep me at the edge of consciousness through prodding, titillating, kidding, and loving me; someone who by constantly reframing my reality would help me to see the theatre of illusion in which I am acting, the shadows on the wall; someone who would transform my "problem" into exciting possibilities, and when I took myself too seriously would show me how poignant I am; someone who could guide me through the minefield of my mind with cavalier confidence and joie de vivre; someone who is not afraid. Such a being would be an "elder" whom I could properly honor, and at the same time fully enjoy.

So when people ask me who I think Emmanuel is, for all the reasons listed above, I tell them that he is an adopted special uncle of mine of whom I am inordinately fond.

Emmanuel reminds us that his message is not new. Spiritual messages rarely are. For what we need to know has been said again and again. Yet, as our cultural context shifts, so must the way in which the perennial philosophy is expressed. Because Emmanuel's words are in response to queries put to him at recent lectures and workshops and interviews, and because of his sensitivity to our predicaments, the material is timely and appropriate to who we are and where we find ourselves.

Emmanuel's message of choosing love over fear and of being an openhearted witness to the way of things, is so simple that I was initially dubious as to whether a second book would be useful or merely redundant. I knew there would be more of his wonderfully cryptic one-liners like his "Death is absolutely safe" line in the first book. And so there are, for example, "No one gets an award for sitting in bliss." A few such lines, while absolutely delightful, seem insufficient justification for a book.

But reading this material has put my concerns to rest. There is a progression from the first volume to this one that suggests that as Emmanuel's audiences, channel, and editor are ready, a more uncompromising version of truth comes forth. As Emmanuel suggests, he is accompanying us on a journey from rigidity to yielding, from sternness to softness, from fear to love. And as we become more comfortable with the initial strangeness of being spoken to as souls on a journey rather than as personalities, the transmission can be more direct.

So much of what we hear in our reading of Emmanuel, or any other spiritual text for that matter, is dependent upon our readiness: having ears to hear. For example, twenty years ago my Guru, Neem Karoli Baba, told me that I need fear nothing and that I should love everybody. For me that turned out to be easier for me to say than to do. I taught that message in writings and lectures but still could only barely hear it myself. But over the years, slowly, slowly, keeping my Guru in my heart, repeating these injunctions to myself as almost a mantra, and deepening my philosophical and meditative understanding of the cosmology out of which such truths spring, I have noticed a dramatic reduction in my own fear and an even dramatic increase in my own love for others.

At first that love was experienced in relation to friends and fellow seekers. In recent years, however, the field in which I experience intense love for others has expanded to include people I meet on city streets and in a variety of situations where previously the experience of love would seem out of the question.

Coincidental with this feeling of increasing love for others came a diminution of fear. To my surprise I found that in places where there was danger, I was cautious yet increasingly unafraid. Most recently this has happened on the streets of New York City, where I spent several months working with the issues of homelessness and lack of housing. I found myself in a number of situations where previously I would have experienced not only wariness but fear. Yet, to my surprise, there was no fear, only quite intense love. In fact, time and again I was overcome with states of ecstasy right on the streets and in the subways of New York. It was that experience which prepared me to really hear Emmanuel in this material when he says:

"Just be aware of your loving. Do that and watch the change. See faces light up. Notice your cities becoming safe. Feel the kindness of your world. You need not say or do a thing. The power of your love will transform every corner."

Had I personally not been through these transformations, I would have read Emmanuel's words without an experiential referent, and I would probably not have received these words as openly into my heart. As it is, however, the words are luminously clear and valid because I hear Emmanuel speaking directly to my own experience. I was, so to speak, ready.

This particular example reminds me of another interesting reason why Emmanuel's words are so valuable to us. As I said above, when my Guru told me to have no fear and to love everyone, I slowly began to change in a profound way.

This effect was in contrast to the noneffect on me of admonitions given by a previous teacher. In discussing this at one time, I recall my Guru asking me if I had given up some habit that my previous teacher had told me to give up. I said that I had not made any headway at all in relinquishing that specific habit even though my previous teacher had stressed again and again that I must give it up. At this point my Guru laughed and said, in effect, "How can his words affect you when he himself has not given up such things?"

This story comes to mind when I hear myself admonishing others to let go of fear and to open to love, even as I myself am just beginning to do so. I see the subtle way in which the very words I use say one thing but the person saying them conveys something else, because we, as the medium, are our message. Whatever fear is left in me is conveyed along with words of fearlessness.

But when Emmanuel speaks of love and fear he is speaking not from his intellect, nor from his wishing-it-were-so. You can feel that he speaks obviously from the depth of his being where fear had indeed been relinquished and love rules. Such a message of love, delivered from such a place of truth, is bound to touch us deeply and facilitate real change.

What real change might we expect? I find that Emmanuel's words deepen my faith in the spiritual dimension of life. In doing so they make me feel less vulnerable. In feeling less vulnerable I am willing to risk deeper and more compassionate involvement in life. Through the combination of deeper spiritual faith and deeper involvement in life, I am able to witness from a spiritual vantage point the ways in which my separateness and fear perpetuate suffering.

So Emmanuel has helped me to look again at my ways of dealing with the righteous indignation and pain regarding the unfair suffering in the world, with the anxiety about ecological or nuclear destruction, with fear of my own death, with the drama of relationship, with how I integrate pleasure seeking with spiritual thirst, with the role of intellect, and with the root cause of my fear of loving too much. To see all these things is to gain leverage over them — which, in turn, loosens their hold over me. This in turn strengthens my confirmation in the spirit. And therein lies peace and joy.

It is, therefore, with delight that I invite you to slowly and reflectively read on in this book of uncommonly good spiritual common sense.

Ram Dass

Fifteen Years with Emmanuel

Fifteen years of incredible challenge and amazing Grace. Fifteen years of becoming more and more gently aware of my human fallibility and my own Divinity. Fifteen years of forgetting and remembering, of falling asleep and awakening. And always there has been this loving presence in my life. I may not always be able to access it, or even to believe it when I do, but Emmanuel promises that no one walks alone. I need to remember that promise a lot, and I know this need is not unique to me.

Emmanuel's teachings come each time with a freshness that delights me. I have learned never to anticipate a response, nor in any manner to put my personal human opinions in the way when I am channeling. My experience is always of loving presence that brings with it a capacity to expand so far beyond mind that my task becomes one of willingness to surrender to the exquisite adventure of the completely unexpected. And this is exactly how Emmanuel would have us live our lives—moment by moment. The fact of channeling itself is to be set aside and the teachings are to be received only if the heart welcomes them. No shoulds or shouldn'ts, no mystery, no "Oh, wow," no blind following, no "one path," just our own loving truth.

The material for this book has been gathered in the many workshops that Emmanuel has led. Each question was asked by the heart of a very real human being. The mutuality of our experience is comforting, dear, and terribly poignant. Every question is mine. Every answer received is of benefit to me.

Emmanuel says we must remember and honor our dreams, our visions. That we must allow them to expand, to create themselves as we grow, but always to be honored in their essence. When I was a child my dream was to embrace the world to make it unafraid. It seems that this is what Emmanuel is doing now. And so my dream is becoming realized through the human delight of traveling with both my dear friend Judith and my husband, Michael, and the meeting and remeeting of the many other dear human beings who come to hear and be with Emmanuel. Can I possibly tell you how grateful I am?

One point I feel is very important. In my personal experience, Emmanuel's teachings really work. What he says he means literally. There are no euphemisms here, no parables, no symbolic language. For instance, his constant reminder to choose love—whenever I remember to do this the entire experience of my life changes. I become more centered, clearer, more open-hearted, more joyous and able to take in the wonders of our planet. When I exhale "all that has ever been" (I personally find this more difficult than the choosing of love), I am free.

And to fall in love with myself, which is his constant reminder, though contrary to all of my life's experiences, becomes not quite so horrifyingly difficult as it once was.

So these fifteen years have affected my life in every conceivable way. It takes constant vigil, commitment, energy, and at times enormous humor to bring it all into some sort of an understandable whole. But I am assured (and so are you) that it is all beautifully possible. We can be human and at the same time unafraid, and the most joyous thing I can say at this point in my life is that I believe him. Some day, so the assurance continues, we will all make it back to our complete remembering of who we really are. I can hardly wait.

Pat Rodegast

In acknowledgement:

The diverse material in this book came from workshops all over the country and abroad as well, once again emphasizing the universality of our human concerns. Some of it is in answer to questions and some is extracted from the mini-lectures with which Emmanuel loves to surprise us.

As Pat and I gathered up those teachings we felt Emmanuel would most want to share, we worked with them over and over again, which allowed us to learn them more deeply ourselves. We would study the meaning, discuss the relationship of one theme to another, and decide how to arrange the teachings into chapters for greatest clarity. Of course, from Emmanuel's point of view, we could just as well have divided the whole book into two giant chapters, one called *Love* and the other *Fear*.

It has been a joy, of course, to be present as Pat the channel spoke Emmanuel's wisdom. It has been an even greater delight to share the excitement of Pat the woman and dear friend as we rediscovered the heart of Emmanuel's jewels as they threw light on some situation in her personal life or mine.

My acquaintance with Emmanuel has brought me a significant reduction in my habitual fear level. In all crises, I find myself "choosing love" as often as I can remember, and the relief is instant. A peaceful heart is a happy one. Working on this second book has been a rich and fruitful gift.

Judith Stanton

Emmanuel's
Book II

1
The Choice for Love

What does the voice of fear
whisper to you?

Fear speaks to you
in logic and reason.
It assumes the language
of love itself.

Fear tells you,
"I want to make you safe."
Love says,
"You <u>are</u> safe."

Fear says,
"Give me symbols.
Give me frozen images.
Give me something
I can rely on."

Loving truth says,
"Only give me
this moment."

Fear would walk you
on a narrow path
promising to take you
where you want to go.

Love says,
"Open your arms
and fly with me."

Every moment of your life
you are offered the opportunity
to choose—
love or fear,
to tread the earth
or to soar the heavens.

Why would fear want to oppose truth?
Because truth has the power to transform fear,
fear believes it is fighting for its life.

I want to say something about the subtle
inroads fear can make in your lives. If you no
longer allow fear to step blatantly before you
and shout of cataclysm, it will creep behind you
and whisper something reasonable in your ear.
Be wary of rational thinking,
reasonable supposition.

Ask your higher wisdom
if it is not true that without worry,
you would have arrived
exactly where you are now,
and more pleasantly.

Doubt is the rabbit's foot of fear.

Worry and fear
are not tickets on the express train.
They are extra baggage.
You were going that way anyway.

How can I know what love is?

By knowing who you are.

How do I learn to love myself?

By doing it. Not by thinking about it. The moment you think about it, you go back into duality, into fear. There you have the whole package neatly wrapped once more in the paper of good intent and tied with a ribbon of the illusion of love. Fear is wearing love's clothing again.

Why do I experience fear of love?

Because regardless of how you begin your opening to love, whether it be to another human being, a pet, a flower, a place to live, or a country, it is a seemingly undefended place.

Love means setting aside walls, fences, unlocking doors, and saying YES.

Are there different gradations of love?

The definition of love alters so readily to suit
the circumstance that the word ceases to have
any definite meaning. Are there different
gradations of love? No. But there are myriad
ways to express it.

Wherever there is love, that love in its essence
is pure. But its purity becomes obscured by all
the other aspects of humanness. It is what you
do with your love in your world that gives it the
appearance of gradation.

The love you are waiting for does not exist
until you allow it to touch you. The blessings
that are all around you in your world cannot
be known until you give them presence
in your life.

There is so much in your world you have not
seen, have not heard. The contracted self
knows only the lens that he or she was given.
What is to be done?

While you are still human, if you would only
allow your hearts to open just so much each
day, to touch your passion, to honor your
loving, you would find an entirely different
world than the one you thought you were
living in. And you would find an entirely
different Self than who you thought you were.

Is there such a thing as unconditional love?

All love is unconditional, and yet it must move through the filter system of human fear. The moment love touches the vocabulary of fear, it becomes conditional. Why?

In your infancy, you were aligned with love in its perfection. When the moment of separation came (and it must in this schoolroom), you realized that you and mother were no longer one. Since you knew that all *you* were was perfect love, the child's mind registered the message that unconditioned love was the cause of separation from Oneness. One walks warily after that with this business of unconditional love.

Does love really transform?

You have no recourse but to try love on.
Be patient, dear friends. You are working with
denser substance than the consciousness that
brought you here. The act of transformation
must be given its time in the world of time.
Fear is tenacious. The intellect will cling to fear.
It has created it.

Illusion has formed your human world. Your
world cannot return to Light until all parts of it
are remembered in the essence of Perfect Love.
Each time you choose love, you transform a
piece of forgetting into remembering. Each time
you honor Self, you allow your life to be lived
fully. The Light of that Self transforms
darkness. Every time you remember who you
are, you take the illusion of forgetting and bring
it back Home. You, as Gods, created this
illusion for the purpose of knowing the nature
of love where love seemed not to be.

As you love, you transform what had not been
loved back into its essence. When the last soul
remembers to choose love, your entire planet
will return Home, and with it every star
you see in the heavens.

Are the stars just here
to serve the purpose of your schoolroom?
Absolutely.
Does nothing exist
beyond the need for love to remember itself?
Nothing.
—and there is an infinity of more.

What might love look like beyond planet Earth?

It looks like a newborn baby
whose eyes are open
to earth and heaven.

It looks like the smile
of someone you love.
And ultimately, of course,
it looks like you.

As love learns to love itself,
it creates itself in its own image.
Your world is populated
by SELF.

2
Fear in Love's Clothing

How can I remain loving when there is so much danger in the world?

You are afraid that justice and love are not all they ought to be. You are afraid that if you were to stand open in love, you would receive violence, mockery, humiliation, and destruction. There are those of you who declare, "The world is real. An eye for an eye." Rules give an illusion of safety.
Structure comforts fear.

Fear says, "Put me in a house with a roof and
locks on my door and I will believe I am safe for
a moment." When you are loving, you are
under the open sky and possibilities are
infinite. Contrary to Chicken Little's
expectations, the sky never hurt anyone.

There are no guarantees.
From the viewpoint of fear
none are strong enough.
From the viewpoint of love
none are necessary.

**How does opening your heart to love protect you from the
violence inflicted by others or the devastation
of a global war?**

Opening your heart to love and *believing in your
choice* makes physical violence and
global war impossible.

Is that an outrageous statement? You seem to be
walking in the most tenuous of times, where
threats are hurled across continents and there
are those who would devastate the planet in the
name of their own fear. You ask yourself, "How
can one human being, with little if any
empowerment, alter this?"

None of you are here to transform your world
single-handed. But the beginning of such
transformation rests with you. When your heart
is open, you are in truth and you remember the
spirit essence that you are. Then what
transpires on this globe cannot limit you.

Fear says, "Wonderful. All I have to do is
choose love and I'm safe." Be watchful. There
may seem to be a million reasons to choose
love, but there is really only one. There is no
other true choice. All else is illusion.

Why do I fear failure?

Because you believe that success is not who you
are; success is something you have to become.

**I feel my fear has a life of its own. I can't control it or
transform it. Perhaps fear needs to be played out. Does
this make any sense?**

Only to fear. It lives on the belief that you grant
it. There is never a circumstance where fear is
not a choice.

My fear of death is overwhelming. It seems so final.

Death is the greatest gift that your schoolroom
offers you. One can assume a bravado and say,
"Of course, I have chosen love!" and beneath
that verbalized choice, fear can still be in
control. But when one actually moves to dying,
fear can no longer hide.

Your fear at this moment is your greatest
teacher. When you have heaped all your fears
into this one undeniable area of human
experience, you will have formulated the arena
within which you can work. Address dying—
fear—where it cannot escape you. It cannot
subtly move away and pretend to be something
else. This may not bring you comfort, but
bringing comfort is not my purpose.
My purpose is to bring truth.

I congratulate you. You have found the illusion
and you have put it where it cannot any longer
delude you. Choose again.

**Someone I know was just murdered. I know in
my head that we choose these things for ourselves, that
we are eternal, etc., but in my heart there seems to
be only terror.**

Chaos is one of the most frightening things that
can be experienced by someone who believes
the only reality is to be found in this world.

Acts of violence that seem to be predicated on
chaos are the greatest opportunities for you to
test your faith. In one manner or another, you
are all destined to leave this world. How your
soul chooses to do that is individual. You
cannot know why a soul would elect such a
thing; you can only know what it means to you.

The act of murder is contractual. It is designed
to serve victim and murderer and anyone else
who is touched by that violence. Walk into your
terror to learn its nature. It will be less painful if
you do not turn away. Stay with the feeling
itself, with no attempt to give it structure. *It is
structure that causes terror, not experience.*
You will see.

I have much less fear than ever. Now I have some concern with not feeling.

That is because you think feeling is fearing. To remove fear, you decided that feeling had to go.

When you are centered in your heart, fear has no power at all. It is something that may scurry through the room from time to time. You need not feed it until it becomes a monster. You can just let it run in one door and right out the other, and you may even comment, "Oh, there goes fear again."

You do not have to mute all things to silence the voice of terror.

Won't I become totally irresponsible when I attain freedom?

Fear tells you that. Don't listen. You might, indeed, be elected President.

Can you give me a mantra to use when I feel lost in my own depression and fear?

You come to bring light where there seems to be darkness, to bring love where fear seems to be. Remember the purpose of your soul. Then such a time of darkness will seem less like an oppressive weight, but rather an opportunity. Where can I see love here?

When, without even knowing the meaning of it, you say with every inhalation, "I choose love here. I choose love," you will see the light change and the darkness dispel. Your mind may say, "I don't understand what happened. All I did was sit here for fifteen minutes choosing love." Well, mind, that's all that is required.

The lifeline, the golden rope, is to know that there is such a thing as love, and in that moment you are empowered to choose it. Just that. Even if your heart is breaking and you feel on the edge of collapse, say, "I choose love." By this mantra you silence the lifelong mantra that would choose fear.

And if fear seems to follow me, what do I do?

Hold fear in one hand. Hold love in the
other. Holding both, choose love and
choose love again.

Fear may call you back, "And what about me?"
You answer, "Yes, fear, I hear you. I choose
love. You may be part of human conditioning
but love will always be my choice, for that is the
only reality." Fear will shout, "But I am truth.
Listen to me!" You reply, "My choice lies
outside of illusion, not within it."

Then watch the pyrotechnics of fear. It will tell you that the plane will crash, the food is poisoned, you will be left alone forever. If you enter into any of those scenarios, you are caught.

Fear is only a teacher on your planet. Your schoolroom is always held within the hands of Perfect Love. All the monsters to be created on your planet have already been unleashed, so fear will have no new faces. Oh, perhaps a virus or two. Nothing more. Fear has emptied out its bag of tricks: nuclear destruction, genocide, cancer, AIDS, torture, and still there is the human heart that seeks to know love.
That is the voice of transformation.
That is the voice of truth.

Fear
is the frightened child.
Love
is the flame
of holy remembering.

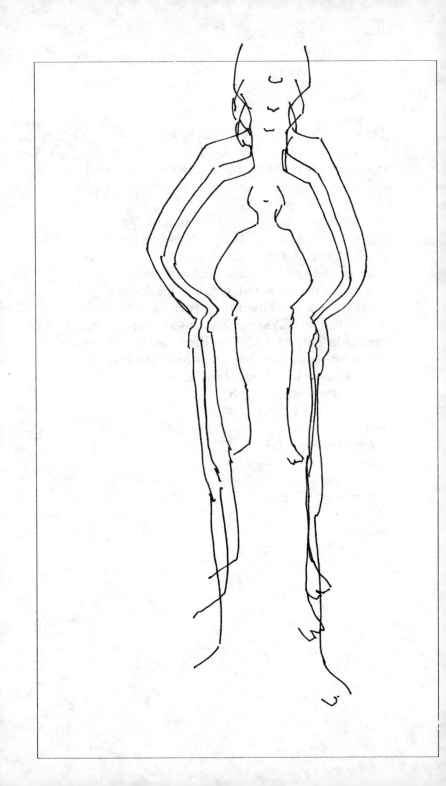

3
Illusion

I would like to discuss illusion. The You in
Oneness and the you in duality seem to be
vastly different. Yet they are not. You might
view duality as a series of Chinese boxes. The
greatest of the boxes is the Oneness. Within
that Oneness is the world of illusion you have
created from Oneness. Within the world of
illusion is the duality. It is not hopeless. Your
world is not opposed to Oneness. It is
embraced by it.

The lenses of your human experience have
altered themselves to the mind's demand, to
fear's preoccupation, to the child's education.
There is another lens available to you, which
sees even your moments of greatest stress,
greatest division and fragmentation as simply
part of the Oneness.

I am held in suspicion at times by my channel
when I address all things disguised as tragedies
as opportunities to choose love. One might say,
"Why, Emmanuel would walk through the very
gates of hell itself and say that was an opening
to love!" Yes, I would. The moment you choose
love, hell vanishes. It becomes just another
remarkable structure in fear's domain.

It is not required that you alter your world one
iota. What will bring you peace is to
alter your perceptions.

You are all ensnared in illusion, much as if you were walking through a field of brambles. You entered the field, called by the beautiful wildflowers there. As you began to walk, to pick the joys, the beauties of this world, you found yourselves more and more entangled in the thorns, until you became so focused on the thorns that you quite forgot why you went into the field at all.

Because your world is your schoolroom, you walk it with a certain amount of respect. That is appropriate, for unless you enter into the illusion, the illusion cannot serve you. At the same time, you must be aware that you have chosen this walk.

Even your bodies are not what they seem. What appears to be solid is, in fact, no more solid than the air. It is only molecular structure spinning exactly as your solar system spins. The vastness of your galaxies is mirrored in the cellular arrangement of your bodies.

Your intuitive heart is the doorway that stands between the worlds. In your willingness to go against all reason, all defenses, all habits, all patterns, all superstitions, and many teachings to say, "I will love," you walk in the Light. You honor the illusion but you will never become lost in it.

As children you have played at putting your hands in front of a bright light and watching the shadow figures on the wall. This is a clear analogy of your life.

Do you choose to look at the shadows on the wall and say, "This is reality," or are you also aware of how those shadows were created and of the brilliant Light that stands behind all illusion?

*Not only are you
the shadow
that is dancing on the wall,
but you are the hand
that makes the shadow,
and you are the Light.*

The image the mind presents of the purpose of human life is limited. The mind has been taught at birth to contain itself and to rest itself in time and space. Yet the mind holds the capacity to exist beyond time in the Eternal Now.

There is a wisdom within you that knows beyond knowing, that will not yield to the linear structure of thinking. Your task is to free the mind from linear bondage by setting the mind to serve the heart, and to be in the Now, moment to moment, in whatever manner the heart will be served. Through that Nowness, the mind will learn its power.

When the child is given alphabet blocks, he is given infinite possibility of communication. When he is taught the concepts of spelling, he is given limitation.

Is mind the enemy? Not at all. The mind has been instructed in the name of fear to utilize the experiences of the world to make you feel safe. Safe from what? Safe from one's own creation? Such illusion, such suffering!

The mind is a doorway through which you walk to live within your world. It has the capacity to make sense out of illusion. It is the tool you have chosen to keep you effectively and effective in your world. It walks you to its expected limit; then you must leap beyond.

What is true intelligence?

True intelligence is the capacity of the mind to honor the wisdom of the heart. True wisdom does not necessitate intellectual vocabulary.

You all have wisdom. You all know everything there is to know, but you have not been given training or permission to express your wisdom in your world.

Is there no form of education other than direct experience that isn't harmful?

First we must define education. The learning of certain formulae of means to communicate— writing, reading—opens doorways to perceiving the nature of your world. These useful skills become harmful when fear intrudes. Anything that one can learn has value as long as you do not give it precedence over your own knowing.

The distractions of your world are enormous. You are taught so early to look outside yourself for verification of who you are, or that you exist at all. You are constantly moving away from the Self.

So once an hour ask yourself softly, "Am I here?"

You have become caught in the illusion
that your identity
rests with your capacity to struggle.
It does not.

Your true identity
is awaiting you
beyond effort.

The key to remembering
is to remind the self
not to be afraid of anything
anywhere
anytime
ever.

Illusion cannot destroy reality.
Can a shadow on the wall
hurt you?

Death cannot kill You.
Pain cannot hurt You.
Disease cannot make You ill.
Years cannot age You.
Fear cannot touch You.
Welcome Home.

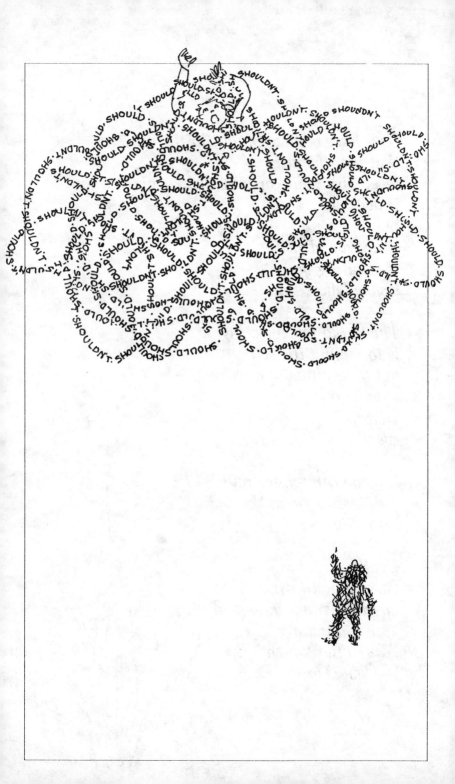

4
The Human Costume

Beneath the reflection
from the mirror of life,
there is unlimited love
and infinite truth.
In each one of you
there is God.

The mind races in and out. It takes Now and compresses it into time and space. The sense of Self is distracted by what you have been taught are the necessities of human survival. You have worn these belief systems as part of your costume all your lives.

The illusions of fragmentation you wear about you are as so much glittering costume jewelry. They capture your attention. Imagine for a moment that we are speaking of physical clothing. You were given an outfit when you were very young which you have altered continuously to fit you. But not quite. Certainly not comfortably.

When you donned the costume initially, there was good reason. You believed that all the memory of Oneness, all the perfect love that you brought was not acceptable. In order to stay alive in this schoolroom, you agreed to wear the uniform. It hid that Oneness you believed was not wanted, and it seemed the only option you were given. Fear took you by the hand and said, "Walk thus clothed and I will keep you safe." The contract was signed, but not in eternal ink. You can break the contract whenever you like. That does not mean that you will not feel fear. It means you will not believe it.

Your loyalty to your costume is touching. Parts of it may even be becoming, but most of it serves you not at all.

Why wear the same clothing that you wore when you were two weeks old? It pushes you into very uncomfortable postures. Where do you think your headaches come from? Your upset stomachs? Your heart palpitations? From the supreme effort of squeezing yourself into something that no longer fits.

Your costume has become your identity. Every "mistake" you have been taught you made comes from the illusion that you should conform to your costume. *YOU* have never made a mistake.

The selection of your parents was exquisite, regardless of how it may seem to you. The choosing of your life to this point, your life's partners or your decision not to have partners, your work, every physical, mental, emotional, and financial experience you have had have all been, from the viewpoint of your soul, remarkable in their service to you. Even the tight clothing has served in that it reminds you that you are not comfortable.

A costume is not the safety you believe it is. Let us then begin to explore another way of dressing. Every moment of your life you have a choice—to bless and embrace your world or to deny it. In the vocabulary of the ill-fitting costume, you deny your world. When you undo this or that tight button so you can breathe, you embrace your world. You *are* your world.

Even your name is part of your costume. Never allow yourselves to be identified with name. Truth cannot be named.

Ultimately you will all stand naked. No shielding is required. You are beautiful in your selfhood.

Be present.
It is your presence that is required in your world,
not your costuming.

You spend your lives waiting for THE KEY
to come to you through linear concept.
That can never be.
All that you have ever been, you are.
All that you believe you must know,
you already know.

You have lost nothing.
In deference to your human society
and the infant's belief in its survival needs,
you have pulled the curtains down.

You live within the confinement
of what you learned is safety.
Behind the shutters of childhood's fear
there waits for you the lighted universe.
It is your Self.

*All that has transpired in your lives
has been designed to bring you
to this moment
and the next
and the next...*

*Oneness can never be fragmented.
In your eternal wisdom,
you are, always have been, and will ever be
whole, one, eternal and perfect love.
There is nothing else to be.*

*God manifests
in many diffferent forms.
You, in your humanness,
have clothed Divinity
in uniqueness,
but you have not altered
its nature.*

Divinity is One.

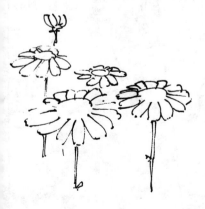

5
The Quagmire of Vocabulary

Why am I here?

This is everybody's question verbalized in one manner or another to suit your personality.

Which "I" are you referring to, the Self of spirit just before you were born, that of childhood, of maturity? The self of fear or the Self of Love? Can you see how, in allowing nonstructure, you open to infinite possibility?

Why are you here? What part of you is asking
that? When you ask the question, be clear
where it comes from. When you have found the
where, be willing to change vocabularies,
to alter meanings.

You are in this world to expand beyond the
sense of self that you were taught.

As children you are taught language. You are
not taught experience. From the moment that
you begin to reach out to learn about your
world, you are given a definition so limited that
it takes the truth of your experience right out of
your hands and alienates you from who you
really are. Your language keeps you captive.

You are in the world, from the viewpoint of
spirit, to recognize that illusion has not the
power that Love has and,
therefore, that Self has.

Could you say more about creating a new vocabulary, one that can describe that which is indescribable?

First we must all be willing to relinquish the illusion that a structured, understandable world is a safe world. Are you willing to do that?

Let yourself experience a world you do not know. Do not give definition, shape, form, or structure to your nonknowing. Let the only thing that exists be the experience of self at this moment. From this place, no words are needed, none are adequate. Your Beingness will express itself in the vocabulary that is appropriate to that moment.

If words want to come, let them be words of spontaneity, not words that might fill the expectations of the mind. There are entirely new ways to use old words that will free them of their limiting effect. There are entirely new ways of weaving sentences together that will open hearts rather than stimulate intellect.

In whatever manner Beingness seeks to express itself, you must allow it total freedom.

Where do ideas come from? Are they events?

Ideas come from consciousness that has learned the vocabulary of human thought. Ultimately, ideas are events.

As creation creates itself within the confines of the agreed contract of human experience, human shape, human vocabulary, it becomes idea. As idea emerges into mind, you have already begun to create the event.

Since different languages separate people, do you foresee a common language for this planet?

Just as there will never be one song that the entire world sings, there will never be one language that the entire world speaks exclusively. There is beauty and vitality in each individual language. By listening to the various cadences, even without knowing the words, you can begin to sense who people are.

Language, in itself, is not the cause of national distrust, but the differences can magnify disharmony. One day there will be one language that everyone knows, and that will honor the unity of your planet.

**What is the best way to recognize the mind
and its limitations.**

The mind is wily, is it not? Mind has learned to
behave as though it were feelings, faith,
or remembering.

The mind has been taught it must live in
structure. It believes it must serve fear. Mind
takes its eternal knowing and puts it into the
vocabulary of linear illusion. So it is the
vocabulary that must be reoriented. Linear,
logical, and frightened—if any of these qualities
are present, you know the mind is involved.

The greater truth is beyond words. The greater
truth liberates mind. The greater truth is simply
the is-ness that is your Self.

Your entire human experience rests with you.
You need to develop the capacity to understand
beyond the language of your world.

And in that way
you will hear
what each crystal
has to say to you,
what each drop of water,
each leaf, each insect, each creature,
and ultimately, what the heart
of each human being
has to say.

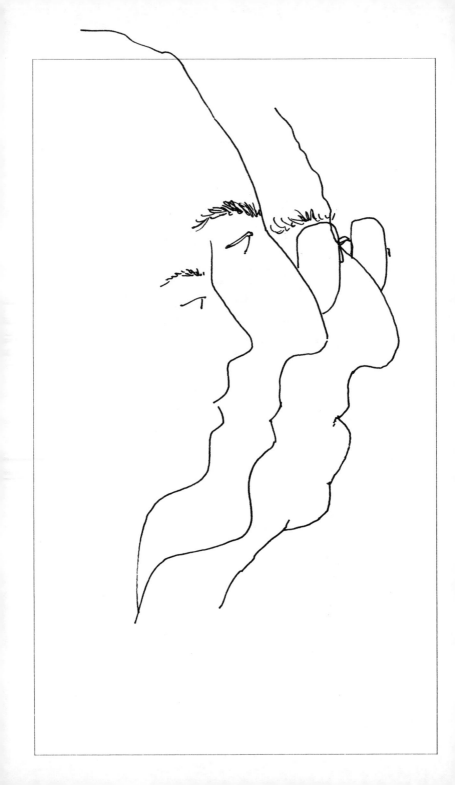

6
Seasons of the Mind: Youth, Middle Years, Old Age

Youth

Emmanuel, how young am I?

You are an eternity
plus half a second.
You are all ages
and no age.

You are born
every time you breathe
and you have lived forever.

Do you see how foolish
a calendar is?

I call this chapter "Seasons of the Mind," not
seasons on a calendar. I added the subtitle,
"Youth, Middle Years, and Old Age," only to
align myself with your theories of what it
means to be human (and theories they are). If
you were to say to me, "Oh, Emmanuel, this
physical body I am sitting in is no theory!" I
would say to you with all the kindness in the
universe, "But it is." Your body is no more than
a glorious thought—God's thought and, by
extension, your own.

Most of you have accepted the illusion that you
are this body. That means your spirit, your joy,
your creativity must now yield to the illusion of
time and space. Somehow you have put things
backwards. You have forgotten that your body is
your own creation.

You have been taught that at a certain age, certain things must happen. You have been instructed so deeply that every cell of your body responds to this belief. It begins in infancy. You are too young to stay up; you are too old to cry; you cannot go to school until next year. Everything is predicated on age.

How can you challenge this illusion? By becoming aware of the limitation time and space impose and taking the courage of the creator in your hands to erase that boundary. Ingrained habits may be difficult to break, but not impossible.

The learned behavior of this business of living is obsolete at the moment of Now. You are reborn whenever a new concept is allowed to enter. All that has been there before shifts and moves and rearranges itself to allow for the infusion of the new. Welcome one new thought, one new idea, one new experience into your life and you are absolutely different than you were the moment before.

Knowing that your human theater is illusion does not rob it of its power to teach you. You will not undermine your creation. You will endow it with a feeling of comfort, a transparency, knowing that at any moment the deepest Self can alter anything.

The moment I can stir the embers of your remembering of what it is like to be beyond time and space, the entire human drama becomes transparent.

If we give up our belief that we are what our childhoods made us, how else can we relate to those same formative events and parental forces?

With loving understanding
and with humor
from the heights
of your own knowing.

With joy and gratitude
for having been given,
clearly and beautifully,
the lessons you have chosen.

With compassion,
as God relates to all things
He has created
in the Name
of His own Love.

Middle Years

As long as you agree
there is time and space,
wherever you are
on the calendar of this lifetime
you are living the middle years
because you are living
between past and future.

I would like to offer you a question. If there is
no beginning and no end, where is the middle?
Oh, I know your calendar and your clock
represent limited time and limited space, but
there is a portion of you that is wiser than that.

The bridge between the past and the future is
all you have. If you insist upon linear time, you
will find yourself running from past to future
and future to past over the bridge that will
not let you rest.

I am not here to convince you that your linear
time has no value. It has its reasons. I do not
want to discourage you from involvement in
your human experience—only to sketch the
framework within which this experience is lived.

I speak from the total Oneness and I speak
from the Eternal Now. Although I address you
in the vocabulary of time and space, I am not a
bridge, for I do not go from one time-space to
another. I exist everywhere simultaneously. You
too exist in the same manner. I stretch you thus
because I want to remind you of who you really
are. Hear me on as many levels as you will allow.

I would not imprison you by addressing you
only in the language of your cage. I love you
from the Eternal Now. I will not enter into your
illusion to do battle with your fears. I would,
instead, free your minds. Read what I say, not
as sentences spaced in time, but as a completed
concept. In that manner, you and I meet both in
your world and in mine.

Who do you think created time? You did. Am I
saying you can reverse the clock? Am I saying
that you can become less in years than you are?
Do I mean that the physical body will alter? If
you want it to and if you can remove the
illusion, the fear, of course it will. I speak of
releasing the chains that tie your identity to
illusion. I advocate the destruction of the calendar.

**There seems to be a wonderful revolution that comes in
these middle years. Can you speak of this time?**

The culmination of your use of the time–space
continuum is that you move from the weight of
subjugation to parents, school, the world at
large, to a lighter recognition that there must be
something rather useful about you after all,
something valuable.

There comes a turning point when you look
around and say, "I really might be all right."

*At that moment
the doors open
and life moves in.*

Old Age

Since there is no time
why am I speaking
about old age?
Why indeed?

When we speak of "old age," we refer to the physical part of you that has been programmed to behave as it "ought to" in the schoolroom in which you have matriculated.

The vocabulary of human experience is predicated on limitation. Though this vocabulary may hold words such as *vastness, eternity, cosmos,* and *God,* the conceptual image of those words is cramped. One believes there must be a beginning and an end even to the endless. Test yourselves. Can you picture endlessness?

When you come into this plane of consciousness, you wear the belief system of boundaries. You can push beginnings and ends to eternity, but they always creep their way back. That is the nature of humanness.

It delights me to remind you of several things: you are eternal; your soul-Self has created this physical body; if you do not choose to remain enslaved by the illusion of time, you need never grow old at all.

If you were to become convinced, without a shred of doubt, of what I have just told you, you would enter the realm of optional functioning of physicality. Yet you would not choose to remain physical forever. It is not necessary and it would eventually become uninteresting. Nevertheless, you hold that power.

When you can return in memory to that precise moment when sperm and ovum came together, you can, because time does not exist, reprogram the cells for perfect and eternal health.

How can I deal with the fear of old age?

Fear has caused you to ask that question, but the same question will, if you allow it, lead you to the central purpose of your life, which is to choose love.

In accordance with the custom of human experience, one is expected to move through childhood, puberty, and adulthood, middle years, and into old age; and if one is good and obedient, one will do that.

If, however, one believes that the dictates of human society do not require such obedience, there is no telling what you will do.

One cannot move beyond structure in the name of fear. As long as you fear old age you are captive to it.

Now, am I telling you that if you learn to love yourself, it won't matter how old you get? Of course. I also want to point out that when fear leaves you, the body is relieved of an incredible burden. Your entire physical system then can maintain a harmony that fear had been disrupting. Fear is the necromancer who takes a functioning, beautiful physical being and transforms it into precisely what you fear.

Your bodies have been taught carefully what
fear expects of them and they obey. Why would
they not? They are your creation. Has your
body been taught what love would allow? A
sense of safety will neutralize the aging process.
Develop the capacity to allow life and remain
on the edge of rebirth as your life unfolds.

One does not confront aging. One recognizes
fear. Aging is merely another place to put it.

If you experience your fear and ultimately
choose love, at that moment the aging process
stops. You no longer require it.

Let me stretch your imaginations.
When you truly choose love,
you do not even have to die.
But you cannot choose love
to avoid death.

It is a subtly devised schoolroom
you live in.
It is demanding
and will not be circumvented.

So what do I tell people when they ask me how old I am?

Tell them, "I am light years old."

And if they ask me when I was born?

Tell them, "I was never born."

Do you all believe that you began to gain your consciousness in the womb? Birth is just a doorway. It has absolutely no effect on the essential being that you are.

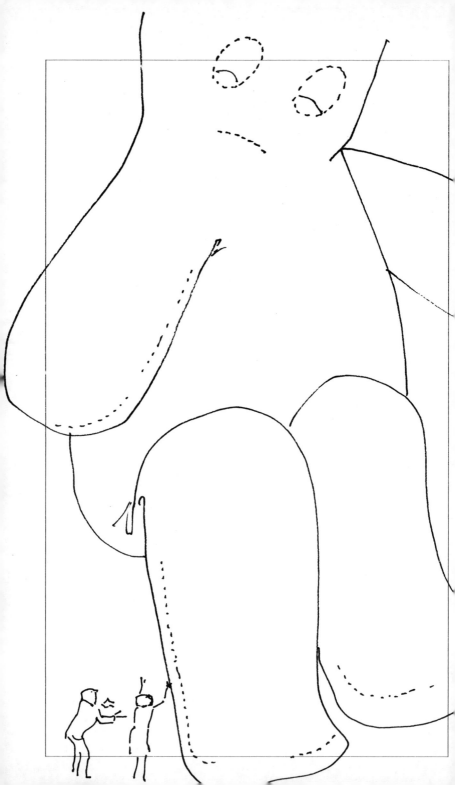

7
Dragons and Other Dilemmas of Being Human

What will I be when I grow up?

When you truly grow up
what you will be
is free.

Sometimes I worry that I am not at the point in my life that I should be. It makes me feel unworthy.

Has God shown you a schedule?

There are no time limits.
Beyond the mind's demand,
there are no shoulds or shouldn'ts
in the universe.

It is as though
you have all, collectively and individually,
created a very large stuffed doll.
It sits on a throne, massive.

As you walk by, you bow
and ask of this doll,
"How am I doing?"

The stuffed doll,
programmed, of course, by you,
shakes its head and says,
"You're really not doing very well at all."

Because you have forgotten
who has created this idol,
you tremble, you beat yourselves,
you suffer, you become ill,
and you die.

The moment of death
is also a moment of remembering.
I cannot tell you how often
you dear ones have left your bodies
and begun to laugh.

What do I do with my old anger? What are emotions anyway?

Emotions are not feelings. They are the vocabulary you have been taught to express what you believe your feelings are, but the moment you move to emotion, feeling is not there. The self of feeling has yielded to the false authority of behavior. Your feelings are your beingness. Your emotions are the learned vocabulary of personality.

Feelings are quiet and profound. Emotions are the pyrotechnics to which you have become accustomed.

Old anger believes it must be a display in the heavens to justify its delayed expression. True anger of the moment gives the self permission to say "no." Then "no" becomes the gentle voice of love.

**But my anger feels like a fire-breathing monster within
me. I am afraid of what might happen if I ever let it out.
How should I handle this?**

Monsters such as you describe are very dear.
They huff and puff and make a terrible noise so
that you, the small child, will feel empowered.
The child says, "You see, if I really, really let this
fire-breathing dragon out, you would all burn to
a cinder. My anger is so powerful, my
disappointment so great, and my displeasure so
vast that if I were only to say to you, 'Look out,
I'm opening the cage to the dragon,' you
would all flee. I would be victorious—and
I would be alone."

Because you did not want to be alone, you kept
the dragon inside. You enjoyed the thought of
frightening your parents (what child does not?),
but the truth of the matter is that your dear
dragon, if let out of its cage and measured, is
probably at most three inches high. It has been a
faithful friend, for it did exactly what you asked
it to do and has been loyally fulfilling the needs
of the small child that you were so you could
sleep at night. Dragons in fairy tales are really
the child's longings, costumed and hidden away
for fear that if they were visible, the child
would be abandoned.

How to let the monster out now when it seems to
be such a roaring fire of consuming rage? Just
open the door.

What is guilt?

Guilt is second judgment. It is looking at oneself in hindsight and saying, "I really ought not to have done that." But, my very dears, if you *really* "ought not to have," you would not have.

Know that at the moment of happening, it was all appropriate. If you have learned since that the act was not what you would choose now and you feel guilty, know that the act itself has brought you to this understanding. That was all it was meant to do.

Why is today's sexual energy so complicated—divorce, disease, etc?

It is not sexual energy that is complicated. That energy is truthful and clear, but it has been required to flow through such muddied and convoluted channels.

Sexual energy is waiting to be honored. Your bodies are vessels of love. There is not one part of you that is not designed to honor love. When you open your heart, you open your Self. Do not separate yourself from portions of who you are. That is fragmentation. That is illusion.

Is sex between two spiritual people a downer on the path to enlightenment?

Nothing on your planet is a downer, certainly not the sharing of physical love. Your bodies were designed to honor love, so much so that the very gateway from Oneness into the physical world is created by physical love. There is no other way to get to your planet!

Your bodies are programmed in the womb, before the mind touches them, before society adjusts them to its own fearful pattern.

Your bodies are designed to dance, to dust the consciousness of God with the lightness and flexibility that will allow joy in your world.

When you move into the physical dance, ask yourselves, "Where am I afraid to be who I am in my own body? Where am I a wallflower at my own dance?"

And by the way,
when you move into your physical loving,
as you remove your clothing,
take off your mind as well.
It simply is not equipped
to hear the music.

How do I work with my judgments? Do I just forgive?

Recognize that every judgment is a self-judgment, regardless of how you spin it around.

The concept of forgiveness lies outside of the Oneness, for it holds the connotation that something wrong has been done. The world is a mirror for you. What is there to forgive?

My deepest fear is of rejection.

The only rejection that has any power is self-rejection. You have been taught that life must define your experience rather than that your experiences are creating your life. You look outside to seek yourself.

Your inner experience is holy. Why then do you look into the eyes of others who hold their own inner selves in question and ask them, "Will you please tell me who I am?" They cannot even know you. How can you give them the power to cancel or amend you?

One creates one's reality. Yet where does one take responsibility in a physical sense? For example: does one believe one's house is safe and not lock the door? Does one believe one is safe in a car and not wear a seat belt?

There is a fine distinction between challenging the laws of your world and self-loving. You have chosen to be human, therefore you walk on your planet subject to its laws. When it rains, you carry an umbrella, unless you want to get wet. When you are hungry, you find food. When you are tired, you sleep. These things are part and parcel of your human world.

The more you remember Oneness, the more you are willing to live fully in your world. As to locking your house and wearing a seat belt, can you honor your world and its illusion without fearing it?

If you know you live in a neighborhood which has spawned desperate people who will, perhaps, break into your house, can you see the wisdom of locking your door while still loving? Seat belts, of course. As long as you are in a physical body, it is self-loving to take care of it. You honor yourself by securing yourself.

What happens when we come together in violence and someone is robbed or murdered? Is *that* in the name of love?

Yes. I do not ask you to rejoice if someone attacks you. You are human. But I ask you to remain in the expanded Self as best you can.

There are no moments that ought not to have happened. Nothing comes about by chance. The design is perfect. Why? Because you are the designer, and you go on creating your lives as you breathe into them.

But how do we handle the monstrousness of some crimes? They seem to cry out for vengeance, yet the way we treat criminals only builds fear upon fear.

This is a great challenge. When there is a closed heart, there is pain throughout the entire universe. For when one has forgotten to such a depth that one would harm another, then the very heavens are darkened by that forgetting. And yet, though the human being in fear cries out for vengeance, there is a deeper knowing that would simply weep for the agony of the loss of love.

Then what would happen to those who have done such terrible things? Oh, they must be protected from themselves and society must be protected from them, but not punitively. Punishment is born of fear.

Am I asking you all to be saints? No. I am telling you that you all *are* saints, that you have the capacity to love in such a way.

Why do karmic lessons always seem so punishing?

Because you believe they must be so. You perceive yourself as unworthy of kindness, undeserving of the bounty that the planet, your creation, offers you.

You will say, "But, Emmanuel, some things cannot be considered as bounty!" I must answer, "Yes, they can." Your task is to utilize everything regardless of its nature, no matter how the world labels it, as a mirror for your own introspection to help you find those pieces of God within you that are hiding.

You honor the world completely when you use it for this purpose.

How do we respond when terrible things happen to us?

Let yourself go beyond the definition of the
person who has had these things happen to him.
The identification one receives from the
circumstances of one's life can be seductive.
You may have experienced this, but this is not
who you are.

Your mind may never know why you have
chosen such things, but you are not your mind.
Your soul will keep its promise to Itself—
the promise of return. Trust in the peace
of that knowing.

I don't understand why people become senile.

Senility is the answer to the soul's prayer. More
often than not, its advent sets the heart free.
When the mind has been rigid and controlling,
there is a time in some souls' choosing in which
they say, "I want to use the rest of this particular
physical existence to recognize my entirety
without the interference of my intellect." And so
the mind is quieted, slowly by some, rapidly by
others. The body can slouch, the mouth hang
open, the eyes wander, and thoughts come and
go without conscious recognition.

Released, at last, from the confines of the tightly
controlling intellect, the heart can soar.

Why are there different races of humans on earth, and when will racial prejudices end?

There are different races on the planet Earth because there is prejudice, not the other way around.

Fear says, "You have skin that is darker or lighter than mine." Rather than moving with the heart that adds, "And isn't that beautiful?" fear says, "Aha, we have something here that is not exactly like us. Let us hold it in suspicion."

Prejudice is simply another language of fear.

How do I remain centered in the midst of child care and the daily stuff of life?

You only become harried when you believe that external stuff is more important than internal stuff.

Do not look ahead and do not look behind. Be in the moment. If you are in child care, you are in child care. If you are cooking, you are cooking. If you are posting letters, you are posting letters. That is all.

If you will allow experience to be full moment by moment, you will be amazed at how pleasant and how much of a meditation that busy flow can be.

What can I do about my fear of not having enough money to fulfill my dreams?

If you believe your dreams are worthy only of the vocabulary of cash flow, I would advise you to reexamine your visions and give them more majesty.

What you love to do, you do well. What you do well will earn you money. If there is not a formal occupation that honors your vision, then I would say it's about time you took your creative power and designed a job for yourself. Is this fanciful? Not at all. Look back in history. Those who amassed great fortunes did not follow in the footsteps of structure. They moved with their own creativity. What brings you joy will bring you abundance.

**How does work imprison or set us free? It is such an
important part of our lives.**

To some of you most of the time and most of you
some of the time, the need to make a living
seems a tyrant. As with all things, work is
another opportunity to find the Self. The
workplace allows you to challenge illusions,
come face-to-face with a great many fears and to
find the gifts and talents that you have.

You have come to this planet first to transform
your own inner landscapes, to remember and
love who you are. From that moment on, you
bring Light where darkness seems to be and
bring love where fear seems to be. That is the
sole purpose of being human. You are all in the
business of transforming your planet.

That is your *real* work.

**Does concern about money stand in the way of
spiritual progress?**

Money doesn't stand in the way of anything. Fear
will make itself known through money concerns.
Because money and fear are both so prevalent,
they have naturally wedded. If you step out of
fear, you will find that money holds no power. It
is simply a means of exchange—pieces of paper
and bits of metal.

If money were not such a useful place to put your
fears, you would find something else. The oxen
would have sore feet, the horse would break a
leg, or the winter would be extra severe.

I would like to discuss abundance.

The universe cannot be miserly. It cannot be wanting. It holds nothing but abundance. It is perfect love, and perfect love is absolute, eternal giving.

How do you translate that into the vocabulary of your world without being accused of being greedy, withholding, or just too wealthy to be bothered with? The world believes it is poor, and in that belief, the wealthy are seen as "other."

One illusion says, "If I am wealthy, I must somehow give it all up." Nonsense. As long as wealth does not own you, it is a marvelous tool. It gives you time; it gives you a sense of well-being; it allows you to help others.

*Another illusion says, "Everything is
limited." You believe that if you have
much, somebody else must go without.
You will find if you allow the world to give
to you, you take from no one.*

*One person walking in the abundance of
the universe will be the Light of salvation
to many who believe it is not possible.
Someone must live the truth. Someone
must tell the Emperor he is not wearing
any clothes.*

*Allow wealth and learn from it. Wealth is
as clear and sometimes as stern a teacher
as poverty.*

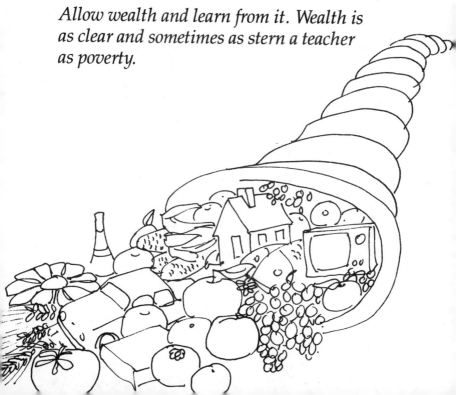

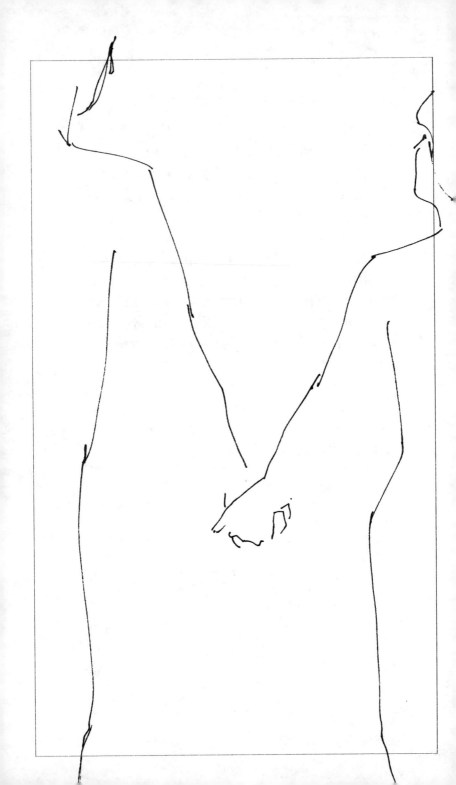

8
Human Relationship

*The subject of relationship
must begin with you.*

You have all seen pictures under a microscope
of cells moving about, all active, all following
their own consciousness. None seem to mind
being brushed against from time to time. They
blend and they separate and they experience.
That's what relationship is designed to be—
freed of the responsibility that you assume for
others or that you insist that others assume for
you. That would clear away a great deal of
debris quite quickly.

Do not single out for special attention one human being whom you would then burden with responsibility for your growth. Relationship is not mutual responsibility. It is mutual love and self-discovery. When two people are bound beyond that, there is servitude and false authority. That is the destruction of relationship.

What can another give you that you, in your essence, do not have? As you look into the eyes of another, your question is really "Tell me who I am, for I have become so embedded in being the perceived that I need you to be the perceiver."

Ask yourself, "Where do I place self-definition outside myself? Where am I awaiting approval? Where have I given over my authority?"

Walk gently, lightly, and joyfully in this life you have chosen—and walk freely.

Please comment on the need for intimacy.

The need for intimacy springs from that portion of you that has been cast from Oneness. It remembers what Oneness feels like and is trying to find its way Home.

Intimacy requires that you release yourself to the moment and stand before the golden door of truth.

If you are living in the past, you are not present.
If you are living in the future, you are not present.
If you are not present, who is?
Without you there is no intimacy.

Please comment on the patterns of relationship that can occur between self and a particular other over the course of many lifetimes? How are these recurring relationships recognized, and how is their purpose fulfilled?

Recurring relationship is recognized just as you have intuited, by seeing a complete stranger and saying, "I know you." Perhaps you bump into someone and realize that your entire life is designed to bring you to that moment.

Once you have loved, you always love. Love finds itself again and again until all things are recognized as Self. Loving relationship goes on to become more and more deeply extended until Oneness is reestablished. Anyone you have loved, regardless of how briefly and no matter how badly it may have ended, you and they are now one. You will know that person time and time again.

Why am I ambivalent with respect to lover relationships?

Ambivalence is a wonderful shield. It avoids commitment in the belief that commitment is dangerous, as one puts aside all defenses to say, "I am here and I love you." That's a very frightening thing when you have not first said that to yourself.

I am in a relationship in which there is much turmoil, and I simply don't know what to do.

Wherever there is confusion (and turmoil is confusion—it's just a little noisier), you know that there is something that somebody, or two people, do not want to see. That does not mean it is worthy of fear. Enter into it. There's a great possibility that just beneath turmoil there is a wonderful oneness that you are both still frightened of.

Ask yourself a question. Where in this turmoil do you find comfort, a sense of identity, and even safety? Letting yourself become lost in confusion allows what seem to be more threatening issues to go unaddressed. To confront these issues with the other in your relationship may seem to create more turmoil, but by that time you will be ready for it.

How do I know when it is time to leave a relationship?

When is it time to leave a relationship? When you don't love anymore. And how do you know that? Ah. That is the challenge. When you are in Oneness, does it not seem there is never a time you don't love? Remarkable. And when you are in duality, does it not seem there is never a time when you love completely? Remarkable.

In relationship you are moving close to the miracle of bringing Oneness into the illusion of duality. Yet how insistently duality tugs at your coattails!

Since love is the entire issue that is to be explored, lived out, and ultimately to be honored in your planet, then love must be the center of the focus. There is no rule that says if a heart has moved, if a consciousness has grown, the human being must remain faithful to something that no longer holds them in the name of society's definition of the meaning of love.

You have not come to do the "right" thing. There is absolutely no way in which you can do the wrong thing, for you have come to question one thing only: "What is the nature of love where love seems not to be?"

Love is not confined to the physical personality, to the human experience. Love is greater than that. People come together to explore love far beyond their minds' concepts or what they could physically discover. Some may come together to find the nature of love when love must leave itself.

Is monogamy the only spiritual way?

Love is the only spiritual way.

I worry about not having a mate, about aging as a solitary person. In my room alone sometimes, it's difficult to feel connected to all life, or even to feel worthwhile. How would you suggest this solitary situation be handled?

Do not be afraid of your loving and your longing. It won't fill your room with loneliness. It will fill your room with YOU and you will not be lonely anymore. Walk with yourself.

Be in the world with who you are, not seeking another, but allowing the world to speak to you. You already know that flowers speak. Listen!

What vows would be appropriate for a remarriage ceremony to celebrate forty years together?

Vow to continue the exploration and your willingness to see and be seen. Join hands again for the discovery of whatever the next forty years will offer. Share in the joy of who you have become, and give more and more of the greatest gift you each have to give—yourself.

Is it possible for two people of the same sex to succeed in a love relationship, or does the sameness of polarity make this nearly impossible?

In the name of love, nothing is impossible.

Do you have any advice for parents of teenagers?

To be a teenager is, unfortunately, to be confined by that label. Do not block off a particular period of time and say, "Now you are a teenager and this is how you are expected to behave."

Teach your children that their gift is the uniqueness of their own loving selves, that nothing need ever be given precedence over that. If society would erase the structures it has placed upon itself in the name of conformity, you would find teenage rebellion a thing of the past.

**How can I keep my own fear from hurting my son? How
can I help him grow up free from fear?**

That is a loving question, but it stems from fear.
Teach your son about fear. To do this, you must
allow him to be afraid without your being
frightened. You can then lead him in his fearful
moments to the very nature of fear, and he will
see for himself that it is illusion.

Teach your son that the only reality is love. If a
child can be taught that each circumstance is
open to the choosing of fear or the choosing of
love, he will choose love because he is still near
enough to the Oneness to remember it.

I have an autistic child. I would like to understand her experience as an "almost unconscious" being.

Dearest one, there are those who would walk on the edge of humanness because they have come only to touch the hem of the human costume. They seek again, after a fearful former life, to reckon how it is that love can enter. How can you understand such a soul? Remember who she is.

Your child comes to you as a wondrous mirror, as a teacher who says to you, "Remember love. Remember who *you* are."

She stands at the rim of human experience— very alert, very aware, a bit reluctant to enter, that is all.

What to say? "You are safe. I bring my heart to you and I will be with you wherever you wish to stand. You are safe and I love you."

**What am I to learn from my relationship with
my mother?**

You are to learn from your mother that there
comes a point when there is nothing more to
learn from your mother. And it's all right.
School is out. But one graduates only with love.

Is there such a thing as a soul mate?

Everyone on the planet is your soul mate. If
there is a man selling newspapers on the street
corner and you are connected to that person
with your openness, your love and truth, you
are with your soul mate for that moment.

I do not mean to destroy dreams, I mean to
expand them.

**Is my father's father's grandfather's mother
my guardian angel?**

Beyond physical reality with all the
ramifications of time, there is only one
consciousness, there is only one time. So the
lineage is unnecessary.

The gifts you receive from the world of spirit
come from perfect love, and it is not necessary
to connect them to family history. If one were to
become enthralled by such a relationship, you
would find, much to your amusement, that you
are born to your children, you have married
your grandfathers, and you have sired your
parents. It would all become so complex that it
would be difficult to live out in human terms.

*Love
will return to love
again
and again
and again.*

9
Politics
and World Events

When we speak of world events,
we speak of all time and all things and all places.
In the greater reality
there is only Oneness,
there is only All-That-Is.

Your world
may seem to be a terribly serious place.
It is not.
What you see
as daily local and global affairs,
from the viewpoint of spirit,
are not happening at all.

I do not mean to diminish
the process of human growth.
It is extremely important.
But hold it lightly.
It is so minute
in comparison with eternity,
where you truly belong.

Why are millions of people in this world living in poverty and oppression? Please don't answer that it is because they choose to or don't believe they can overcome it.

There comes a time when such a viewpoint as "Yes, one creates one's own reality" is so misused that it ceases to have meaning. Any truth misused becomes a half truth, and half truths are far more destructive than absolute fabrication because they bring with them enough of the flavor of truth that one fears to reject them.

Why are so many people living in poverty? Because fear is rampant on your planet, and fear says, "There is not enough and I am going to get all I can because if I don't, I may starve."

Your world is formulated by the consciousness of everyone on it. Some come with the terror that if they do not take from others and stockpile what they may never need, they will be destroyed. Others come in an act of love to offer those who are in such illusion the opportunity to live out their fear.

Poverty is chosen for self-learning and as a gift of love to help others perceive their fear so they can transform it. Do you think each one walks alone in your world? You are all part of the tapestry, and everything you do individually affects the entirety. Your planet is a mutual dream, a mutual creation.

Please say something about the connection of peace to justice. For example, housing, food, human rights, self-determination, racial and sexual equality, etc.

Peace and justice in these issues are the same thing. Then what does one do in a world that is determined to see things in polarization? Have you any idea how much struggle and effort is given century after century to balancing seeming opposites?

Those who are seeking Oneness will walk the path of justice. Do what you can to serve equality, but never for one moment believe in inequality. Within the illusion, do you know how unjust justice is? Inequity lives in history. You do not.

Could you speak about the current crisis of homelessness?

The homeless are everywhere. None of you are Home.

Those of you who believe you have a home are more in illusion than those who walk without one, knowing at least that part of the truth.

Honor the homeless ones as your teachers. Do not look upon them as less fortunate but as more courageous and you will find places for them in your hearts and perhaps places for them in your homes.

If you saw Christ or Buddha wandering the streets, there would be no hesitation. You would open your doors and say, "Come in and honor me with your presence." Would you dare say that to strangers on the street? It is the nonrecognition of the greatness of another human being which renders him homeless.

**Will the present uncertain economy continue in our
Western world?**

As it spins along on its flimsy track, the
economy may suddenly come to a point where
the stock market will not know whether it is up
or down for a very long time. The market will
behave erratically, I believe they say, and the
economies of the world will be draped with
gloomy predictions and mourning.

But there will come a glorious day when there
is an awakening to exchange and sharing. This
will offer an opportunity for introspection and
perception of greater truth for those who fear to
lose and those who fear to gain.

You may ask,
"Are you speaking of socialism, Emmanuel?"
No. I'm speaking of Oneness.
Or "Are you speaking of communism?"
No. I'm speaking of love.

And if that sounds naive to you,
lift yourselves up here a minute,
take a look at your world,
and tell me what is naive
and what is not.

What would a truly spiritual leader be like as President?

The one who sits in that Oval Office would be someone of deep honesty. A human being who says, "We must create an atmosphere where truth and love can abide. For the time has passed for manipulation and control."

Now remember, the mind can conceive of ways to present anything to make it seem true. So the leader of the future must be an intuitive being, a world figure whom everyone respects, whose mind is clear because it is at the service of truth. This is a being of courage, of exciting ideas, of passion, and one who can laugh a great deal at the nonsense that seems to be now regarded as the stabilizing governmental practices of your country. A free soul will guide the world into the millenium.

But what party will he or she run in?

A party of their own.

How will such a person get in?

By popular acclaim.

When?

In eight to ten years.

[Editors' note: We hesitated to include this because Emmanuel seems to have his own interpretation of Earth time.]

Will a woman ever be President in this country?

Absolutely. However, when you say, "in this country," I believe you need to expect that there will be more of a boundarylessness about the world.

**I have a feeling that capitalism doesn't work and
socialism is a failure. Is there a third course to follow,
and what might a new economy be?**

When you all begin to perceive yourselves as
Beings of Light, Beings of Love resting in
eternal safety, government of any obvious
restrictive form will be totally unnecessary.

So what will be the next step? The next step is
spiritual education of the human race, and the
economy will simply be the natural flow of love.
And who is going to be the head of this
government? Each one of you.

I know there are those with political science
backgrounds who are raising their eyes to
heaven and saying, "That is pure idealism. It
will never work, Emmanuel, not in a million
years." And I say perhaps in half a million,
perhaps even less than that, for humanity is
moving very, very swiftly. Give me ten years to
prove my point. Consciousness is moving to the
realization that Oneness, brother- and
sisterhood, are the only ways to survive.

As this is understood, there will be a
committee, not in the tired old form that causes
everyone to groan, but a committed, spiritually
oriented, wise, and vulnerable assembly which
will assume the leadership of the world.

There will be an equal number of men and women on this committee, and certainly, by that time, the illusion that race or color make any difference at all will have dissolved. There will be no one counting heads as to who is white and who is red and who is black and who is yellow and who is brown.

The primary premise will be United Consciousness, United Awareness, United Purpose. This will be a planetary government with its only aim to ensure the opportunity for all to know their own hearts and to follow their own Light. That will be mandated (isn't that strange that one must mandate love?) for there will be many who are just entering the schoolroom. But the leaders will be of the graduating class.

Is civil disobedience a positive tool for bringing about social change?

When love stirs your conscience to say "No"
how can you possibly say "Yes"?

So have at it, my friends,
wherever your heart leads you.
Wherever your truth must be spoken,
speak it in love,
in compassion for those
who yet cannot hear,
for that is what you have come to do.

Speak it with joy
for those who are ready to listen.
Speak from the fullness
of your own knowing.

Civil disobedience? Oh my yes.

Given the state of the world today—starvation in Africa, turmoil in Central America and the Middle East, and so on—what is the best strategy to make things better?

Your entire world is a woven, solid fabric where nothing happens disconnected from anything else. Even war-torn areas serve a purpose. They teach that such running sores need to be healed.

As you learn to perceive with an open heart, what seems to be taking place on the physical plane of your world, it becomes time to speak.

And what are you to say? Why, anything your heart tells you. Whom are you to say it to? Anyone who will listen. The moment that you speak from love and not from fear, you assume the mantle of leadership.

This is not the time to wring your hands and say, "I don't know how to begin. By the time I get things organized a million people will starve." That is not your responsibility.

Your responsibility is to hear your own heart.

This is a schoolroom for learning how to love what appears to be absolutely unlovable.

What can possibly be learned by being a child starving to death in Africa?

Each soul has chosen what will encompass the greatest possible inner soul experience to hurry it on the way to complete self-recognition.

Children have been here so short a time that they have not quite established the habit of forgetting who they really are. We touch them constantly and offer them encouragement. We hold them at night and fill them with love.

This does not mean that it is all right to let others starve in your world. If faith in a bountiful universe existed, there would be an automatic sharing. It is fear, again, that causes people to hold more than they need and thereby create starvation for others.

Are people like Qaddafi afraid or actually biologically unbalanced?

It is amazing how biologically unbalancing fear can be.

What is the likelihood of a nuclear holocaust in the twentieth century?

There are many, many souls, some who are just beginning the journey in this particular schoolroom. It will be a long time before your planet is no longer needed, and when that moment comes, it will not need to be blown up. As part of mass consciousness, your earth will recognize it is no longer required. It will allow itself to return to Light.

Perhaps what is needed here is a brief description of what constitutes physically materialized matter. It consists of consciousness, both individual and collective, that has agreed to manifest in a form that is usable. It is ultimately a dream, but that does not negate its validity for you while you are here. It is formed in the name of love, to serve those who are seeking to know themselves again, to remember what they have forgotten. It is a mirror of the most excellent quality, for whatever you hold within you as the curriculum for a lifetime will inevitably materialize in your life so that you can see it.

You may feel as though these world issues are out of your control. Fear tells you that. But since you are God, and in your loving you are all-empowered, do not believe fear for one moment. However you may clothe it, fear is merely the shadow of forgetting.

Can peace and national pride coexist?

Every country on your planet is predicated on division or it would not call itself a country. The act of placing a boundary represents belief in "other" rather than Oneness.

Peace has no boundaries.

How will the U.S.–USSR conflict be resolved and when?

When you are all sick and tired of listening to it. When the "issues" are no longer important. When a greater matter has superimposed itself.

You know how it is with children. There can be a terrible argument until someone calls them all home to dinner. And then, what has been the subject of most intense emotion becomes a thing of no importance at all. It will amaze you how quickly this issue of controlling the world dissipates when there is an actual circumstance to be addressed.

Then is it all rhetoric?

Not completely. It is based on fear. There is the reality of a stockpiling of nonsense weapons. Yet it bears repeating that every nuclear warhead is a teaching device, an educational tool. The more you perceive them as such, the more you will be empowered to dismantle them—to take them apart one by one and to return them all in their respective pieces back to the earth whence they've come—without toxicity, without fear.

The political systems of the United States and Russia are not conducive to putting into power leaders who live by spiritual values. Yet the world crisis is a spiritual crisis. How can the planet be healed if the consciousness of those who govern is not inspired by a spirit of cooperation and a willingness to serve the common good of all humanity?

The Divine Plan permits the illusion of leadership until the education of consciousness is complete.

With the birth of your planet,
time began.

As consciousness grew
from creative force to its symbolized reality,
the oceans, the winds,
the lightning and thunder,
and into living organisms,
there was a dimming of the ability
to contact the Greater Wisdom.

Then you human beings
came to a crossroad
where there seemed to be
irreconcilable demands:
the United States of America
and the USSR
vying for the privilege
of ruling a destroyed Earth.

You say, "There has to be another way!"
But the "other way" can never be the other person,
the other nation.
The other way is always another way of being
within yourself.

When the greater reality of Self
becomes available again
as it was in the formation of your Earth,
who you are
will transform your planet.

To negotiate from fear is not productive.
To negotiate from love and from mutuality
will create such changes
that it will fairly spin your heads
to see how quickly the world can turn
from separation to Oneness.

Your entire human experience
is predicated on your viewpoint.
Your viewpoint
is predicated on your inner belief system
and that is predicated
on how much you believe in fear
and how much you believe in love.

There is no separate entity called Russia.
There is no separate entity called America.

What form can we expect the evolution of man to take in our future?

The evolution of the species will move from rigidity to yielding, from sternness to softness.

You will move into the planetary compassion you are all seeking. There will be food for everyone. There will be clothing for everyone who wants it. The animals, the creatures of your planet, though they will exercise their own nature in their own way, will become more trusting.

Does it sound like Utopia? Do not be wooed into egocentric somnambulism by this description. There is a great deal of growth required first. Your planet will still be a schoolroom, but there will be more acceptance for its imperfections. You will all smile a lot more.

10
Illness
Is a Doorway

If you jog every morning, eat nothing but
health food, avoid sugar, haven't smoked in
years, make sure you get enough sleep, and
drink only bottled water, yet you do that from a
place of anxiety, you are not in any way
maintaining your health. You are merely not
heeding what it is that will, at some time, make
you ill—which is fear.

Fear is a marvelous motivator. It is never a
solution. It is always the cause of any
discomfort, of any pain, of any illness.

Let us remember that we are speaking of
doorways. We are not speaking of black holes or
endless pits or chasms of despair. We are
speaking of passageways designed to lead from
some place to another place,
not into nothingness.

What is the use of suffering and pain?

Pain reminds you that pain is not your truth.
Suffering reminds you that suffering is not your
reality. The moment you know that, you begin
to transform the illusions of pain and suffering
into the remembering of love and joy.

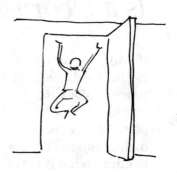

How do we deal with pain?

Pain is given form and shape. Yet it is not a thing. It is an experience. As with all experiences, it can be held or it can be released. But it must not be given shape and it must not be given space and and it must not be given time.

Rather than let it become a bulky, solidified block of consciousness labeled "pain," perceive it as a message running along the nervous system. Let it continue its movement, its flow. When pain is perceived as solid, it becomes agony. When pain is perceived as movement, it lessens.

Therefore, softens. Liquefy. Nothing in your human world needs to remain in concrete. As pain is released into movement, it transforms.

You might start to deal with pain by picturing it as a solid piece of ice. Next envision bubbles of warmth being addressed to that block of ice until it begins to melt and the bubbles are allowed to go through it. Release all concept of what will result. Focus on the process taking place.

Pain does not exist except in history and anticipation. If one could remain in the moment of Now, there would be sensation—without pain.

I feel that it is often my body and illnesses that stand in my way. Could you please speak of ways to feel Oneness through the body?

Your body is not solid. Its structure is a spinning universe. Science knows that the molecules do not even touch. They have as much relative distance between them, as much law and order, as the planets in your solar sytem. What are the spaces in between filled with? What holds it all together? Love. The part you identify as your physical body is a temporary costume.

How do you see the problem of addiction, Emmanuel?

The nature of addiction is fear. So I will deal
with the expression of fear through the
doorways of addiction and illness.

Each one of you, when you are born, contracts a
fatal disease. It is fear. Now, what has addiction
to do with fear? Those of a particular kind of
sensitivity feel they cannot bear this world and
are seeking a way to touch Home. They try to
desensitize themselves or in some manner
remove themselves, and so they find some
substance which seems to offer a breath of fresh
air. Whatever chemical is chosen, it is initially
intended simply as a respite.

There are those who have chosen a physical
body and designed it carefully who find
themselves addicted to some form of escape
until that escape becomes a poison. Then either
the body must die or the human being must
come to terms with the reality of the world that
says, "There is no escape that way." If the soul
is ready to make that next turn, then the one
who is addicted moves into treatment to heal.

Addiction is always a path of awakening.

I have what is considered, in formal medicine, a degenerative disease. It is now taking my eyesight. In the interest of my soul's vision, how may I end the conflict between what is possible (complete healing and rebirth) and what seems to be the slow and inexorable loss of my faculties? My heart seems to see far better than my eyes.

Thank your heart. You have come precisely to learn the clarity of its vision.

Not to sound macabre, but is not life itself a degenerative disease? One of the remarkable things about donning form is that the moment you put it on, you begin to leave it. You have simply taken the matter of earth and dusted it upon your essence, as you would talcum powder, in order to assume shape in this particular moment.

I am sorry you are suffering. I know no rule
that says this must be so. I am sorry there is
fear in the world. That is what you have come
to transform. I am sorry for the forgetting that
causes dark nights of loneliness for all of you.
You have come to walk in the forgetting in order
to move to the remembering again. In dark
nights, in fear, ask your heart, "Is this all there
is?" Your heart knows the answer.

Do not fight to maintain what you believe is the
necessity of a physical capacity. The moment
you truly release it, it returns to you whole.
Release fear and love is there. Where love is
present, all things are possible. I do not speak
just metaphysically, I speak practically as well.
Look to where fear lies and choose love. That is
your work. That is how your body
is serving you now.

Do you see a cure for AIDS in the foreseeable future?

Yes, and it is coming swiftly. So the time is short for you to learn from the manifested teaching that AIDS offers. The moment there is a cure for AIDS, if fear has not been reckoned with, you open the way for another fearful something. There has always been a simple cure for fear—the choosing of self-love.

[Editors' note: Emmanuel said this in the Autumn of 1988]

How many who have ultimately died of AIDS have found along the way the wisdom to begin to love themselves? How valuable a teaching to the soul! Human fear says, "Yes, but they died." Well, they left their bodies. Some have already come again to teach what they have learned. At the moment of dying, or soon before, they came to the realization that they are worthy of their own love. With such empowerment, they return swiftly. The next ten years will see an influx of wise and loving children. It is a far vaster dance than seems apparent in your human world. Remove the lenses of human focus and you will see from the viewpoint of spirit the wonder of it all.

Do not let AIDS drive you into a corner,
forgetting the purpose for which it has come.
AIDS is fear and fear comes in many forms. It
is an energy current in your body. It is a false
belief from childhood. It is an old tape in your
minds. Before the cure for AIDS is announced,
do your homework or you will move to
something else. The learning opportunity
is here. Why wait?

Explore everything, examine everything in your
lives, but always with the question "Am I
choosing love or am I choosing fear?" When
you find that you have chosen fear, move not
one inch further until you have walked through
that fear and found the love beyond. This is
your task. Through the wisdom of your soul, it
can no longer be avoided. You have given
yourself a gift. The only healing is love.

Take yourself tenderly by the hand. Reach your
hand to others only as you become secure in
your self-loving. Never offer a hand to another
in fear. If they are in terror and you feel a
resonating fear in yourself, walk away. Your
task is to choose love, not to serve the fear in
others—an important distinction. Welcome to
the graduate course. You are both professor
and student.

How, then, can we best learn from this disease?

Take a moment to step back and perceive the entire business of AIDS from a vantage point outside it. Whether you have been diagnosed as having AIDS, whether you have just had a child or lover die of it, remain on the fringe of your own terror. Look at the AIDS epidemic as though it were encased in a crystal ball, in a container that allows visibility. What you see is this: an attack upon the immune system of the body that renders it incapable of self-defense. All the elements that are in your world—in your air, your water, your bodies—then become threatening, and you are no longer able to keep them under control.

From outside this framework, what has been in your human experience that you have felt you must defend against? There is no structure required except that you be willing to see, beyond the terror of the fixed focus on AIDS, what its message specifically is for you.

You have not failed when you become ill. When the body takes upon itself an affliction such as AIDS, the human personality becomes an enemy far more destructive than any virus. Because you turn upon yourselves. You close your hearts. You take terror by the hand. Fear, resentment, rage—all of those emotions, even without the virus, will render you helpless.

You have chosen to walk on this particular path, and I do not mean the path to your imminent demise. I mean to WALK ON THIS PATH. Look at the scenery of opportunity and do not for one moment abandon your life. Utilize every aspect of living to perceive wherein the greater design of your soul has offered you the gift of choice—love or fear.

If I were to give you anything in God's Kingdom,
It would be the truth that what exists here and now
is surrounded by an eternity of love and Light
and what you experience in your humanness
is the choice of your soul—not to its destruction
but to its liberation.

How to work with someone who is dying?

See them in the light of what you know of who
they are and why they have come, and you will
ask the appropriate questions to open the door
to their memory. But be very aware where you
are in fear, you are no longer in truth. And
when you are no longer in truth, you have no
business being with somebody who is dying,
because they are expanding into truth,
and they need to move in joy.

Death is not a failure.

How can one with a fatal disease dance out of life when life is considered the only meaningful possession?

And that is probably what made room for the fatal disease. Well, let us first go back to the Greater Reality. Life is fatal. Therefore, everything that you do, if you want to look at it in that manner, is fatal. Being born is the most fatal thing you can do. When one says, "fatal disease," one is allowing fear to displace reality.

There is nothing more fatal about disease than about anything else except the label. Am I being unfeeling? I don't think so.
I am naming the dance.

You are taught you must not dance with death, with poverty, with illness, and you certainly must not dance with pain. You rarely dare to dance with joy. All of these labels keep you locked into the illusion that some things will die and some things will not. When you finally allow yourself to trust joy and embrace it, you will find you dance with everything. Because everything is the same.

How can one dance out of life when one has a fatal disease? Well, one learns to dance in life. Since the entire fabric of your human experience is fatal, you simply dance.

Everything in your life is a process that will bring you from birth to death, from home to Home.

How can I learn to dance
with a terminal illness?
The moment that you ask that question
the orchestra is already tuning up.

Your willingness to explore
is the dance.
Your willingness to seek
is the finding.
The minute you say,
"There is another way to do this,"
you have found the other way.

Trust the portion of you
from where that question came.
Honor it above all illusion
of living and dying in illness

—and your dance has begun.

11
Death:
A Preview

When you enter into the human world,
you believe *you* have been born and will die.
We must move to the definition of dying.
Fear's definitions are familiar and extravagant.
Love says, "I do not know what death means.
In this moment of eternity, I see neither beginning
nor end." In its perfection in the moment of Now,
love sees no death—only that moment of loving.

Sit in those loving moments as they breathe into your lives. Be present with no history and no anticipation, and in the name of love, you will not die. Here we are touching subtleties. Fear has already said, "Oh, good, I have the way out. I will simply sit in love and never have to fear death." In honoring that statement, you bring death into reality. You die every moment you choose fear.

Do you know how many times
you have died?
Not only the emotional deaths
of this lifetime,
which are countless,
but the physical dyings
of past lives.
You may have experienced death
a thousand times,
yet you have never died.

Where did my friend go when he died on Sunday?

Where you go
when you erase the lines
of self-restriction.
Your friend went out of illusion.

Is it always frightening to die?

It is the language surrounding dying that makes
the process difficult. If you will stay in the
moment, you will not even know you have
died. You are eternal. You will move from this
life to the next in a breath. You will probably
have to be reminded, by the spirits who are
there to greet you, that you have left your
physical body. All the fear and all the pain does
not exist beyond the doorway of death.

What you find
is what you pray for
what you remember
and what you seek
your entire life.
Bliss.

What is the process of dying—exactly?

Exactly, dying is a very inexact process. Each
one of you is born uniquely. You live uniquely.
You will die uniquely.

The process of dying is this: a soul's intent in a
human lifetime has been fulfilled and the soul
considers whether it wants to remain and begin
something else or not. It does not matter how
old or young a person is chronologically—
this is the process.

The soul ultimately decides, "I've done all I
can with this particular circumstance. From
here on in it will be unfruitful in some manner
and that will not serve Perfect Love. So I choose
to come Home."

Well, the decision to come Home is the start of
what has been termed "mysterious terminal
illness," "accidental death," or whatever it may
be. It can even be murder. But once the soul
has made that choice, then the body and the
life comply.

At this point, the process of dying becomes much more specific. There comes the time for each of you when even your human personality, in all its fear, concludes that it is just too much struggle to delay dying. You must surrender to it. Though the mind may find that a terrifying moment, the heart is overjoyed. At that moment, Grace enters. At that moment, Peace descends.

When your eyes have become adjusted to the greater vision, there they are—those Companions of Light you love so deeply. They walked you to the doorway of birth and promised you then that they would be there waiting at the doorway of death. And they are. You are Home.

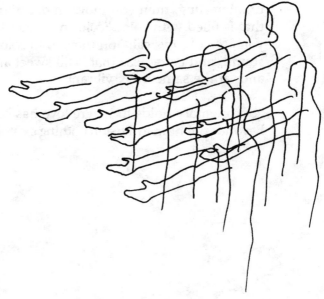

What is the moment of death like? What is it like after death?

You all hold memory of the many deaths you have had. Is it frightening? Not at all. If it is alarming as you walk toward the doorway into death, it is because you have been taught so. Within you there is the cellular memory of being beyond physical manifestation. Each cell in your body is no more physical than you are. It is Oneness moving into physicality and the illusion of separation.

When you finally decide—and of course you must—that it is time to leave, that all of this business of clinging to something that no longer serves you is time-wasting and ultimately uninteresting, then you move into a stillness that is filled with color. Color has sound when you are not physical. You move into color, sound, and beingness that is all sweet and soft and, at the same time, vibrant.

Your memory holds to where love has been. Beyond your human illusion nothing exists but love.

Does one go through a dark tunnel that opens into light?

Oh, I suppose so, if that is what you have been
taught and if you still remain inside your
physical body longer than is necessary after the
body begins to die. Do not demand to see such
an image. If you have decided that it is the end
of this incarnation, there will be an immediate
release. This in no way discredits the reported
near-death experiences. They are different
because the soul did not leave. The tunnel,
then, is the decision to stay. Nevertheless, it is
all very pleasant, just as described.

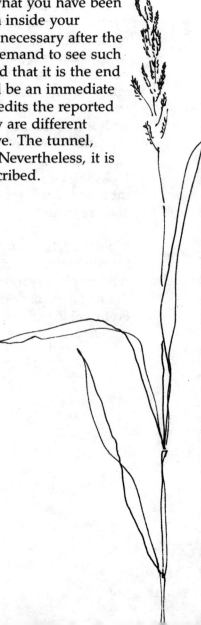

What happens in sudden death?

To the soul, it is bliss. You are driving along in a car doing battle with your life as usual, when all of a sudden you are not. You find yourself unexpectedly light, and you wonder what miracle has taken place. Have you become enlightened that you are no longer immersed in the issues of your day? You look around to realize that the car, which was so important, is now just a heap of rubble and you really don't care at all. Then you see a physical body which looks familiar to you, something you have worn for some years. Yet you are glad to be out of it. You are free.

Violent death is violent only to those who remain behind to view it. To the one who dies, it is simply a wondrous flight Home. All the drama takes place on your side of the doorway. From my viewpoint, the entrance to death is clear Light.

What happens then?

That depends almost entirely on what you expect. Remember, you are the creator of all things. If you expect judgment, very well, you will receive judgment. If you expect to be chastised, then I am afraid no matter what we would like to give you, we have to comply with the Divine laws of creation and give you chastisement. If you expect the loving embrace of those who have left before you, I assure you they will be there with joy. If you expect to suddenly understand the things of the life that you have just left, I believe we can arrange that too.

To understand *all* things, however, must mean that you have completed the reincarnational cycles, that you have awakened all the areas of your consciousness that have been asleep.

The very act of dying does wonderful things for people. It releases them from illusion. You cannot imagine what a relief it is when you finally have accepted the fact that you are going to let go of the physical body. You say, "All right, I'm being squeezed out of this like toothpaste out of a tube, and I simply cannot go back because the body doesn't function." The moment you surrender, it is joyous.

And what is it like beyond this world?
It is very different.
It is much the same
for you take yourself with you.

Those who find the thought
of traveling through eternity with themselves
distasteful
have important work to do.
It is the work of self-love.

You are your best companion
and you accompany yourself always.

That is the only structure I can give you
for the entire universe
is predicated on love
creating itself.

Why have I always been afraid I would die of drowning?

How you fear you will die in this life is not how
you will die. It is how you have died in the
past. When you think of leaving your physical
body, you think of the exit that is familiar. Fear
says, "Well, if we know that's how we're going
to die, then we have control over it, don't we?
We just avoid that or we look at it very carefully
as we walk by, so it remains at bay."

Then the gentle arms of death embrace you
while you are peering nervously at "the enemy"
in the corner. You lie back and sigh, "Ahh, is
that all? Of course. I had forgotten."

You will not die as fear tells you. That is a
promise. Now, what are you going to do with
all that fear which has stood sentinel at the exit
door? It is a vast amount of energy. Where
will you put it?

Let us play with that a little. You realize that
fear has been given false duty. It has been
blocking a passageway you never intended to
use. Fear takes vital portions of your human
personality and gives them sober purpose,
vigilance, and responsibility for keeping you
safe. That is nonsense.

You *are* safe. You would be safe if you walked
without one ounce of fear for the rest of your lives.

There is something else you can do with fear's
incredible vitality. Give it another label.
Call it excitement. Look how much more energy
you suddenly have. Another piece of you
has been remembered.

Please discuss the death urge, suicide, the desire to leave the planet and not participate.

I want to remind you that those who commit suicide recognize immediately the futility of what they believed was the final act of self-destruction and escape. They gather quickly all the details of what happened. Then the wisdom and love that is there instructs, directs, and sends them back to the planet.

The longing for death can, when it comes from remembering, be a voice from Home. When it comes from a desire to escape, then I'm afraid it's only that.

Emmanuel, would you talk about euthanasia? Do I have the right to make that decision for my dogs?

To choose the moment of another's death is an awesome responsibility when it is perceived in that manner. If you will lift slightly above human or animal concerns, you find that in the perfection of the Plan, you are there for that choosing.

Euthanasia is merciful release from a body that no longer functions. In the center of your being, there is no doubt or confusion. Then the voice comes in and asks, "But how do I know this is not a learning process for my animals?" Well, with animals it is quite simple. They do not require a learning process. Animals are with you because they love you. They have not left the Oneness as human beings have and do not need the same complexities of curriculum.

Animals are offering you the dimensions of love you believe are unsafe to give to human beings.

And what about euthanasia for human beings?

Euthanasia for a human being is quite different.
If others ask to be released, they know what
they are doing. If they say, "No, don't release
me," they know what they are doing. If they are
comatose and do not exist at all within the
body, then the decision of what is life and
death and what is the meaning of love rests
heavily upon those who bear the responsibility
for that decision. It is a growth process from
beginning to end.

When does life cease? When the heart stops?
When the brain dies? No. When the will to live
no longer exists.

When you sit in prayer and meditation, you
touch a choice that has already been made. No
one truly is empowered to decide the moment
of death for another. You are only obeying the
agreement. Fear cannot lead you to truth, but
love has never left it.

Could you discuss reincarnation?

Just because you die and are reborn does not mean that circumstances change. You carry the fruitful harvest of your life at the moment of your death into a birth that brings you back into similar circumstances.

Look around in your lives now and imagine inhabiting the same circumstances, holding the same loves, but being newborn.

When you go into the world beyond to rest and to plan and to create your next life, you hold the essence of the remembering you have developed in the lifetime you just left. You then turn again to touch the same point of evolution, perhaps in the vocabulary of a different life.

What will take away our fear of death?

*The wisdom to perceive
beyond illusion.
Then you will know that living and dying
are merely frames in a motion picture,
a light playing on the wall.*

*There is nothing of any genuine reality
in dying or in living
except what is allowed to touch
the loving truth.*

*Death is a doorway
that does not close.
Birth will use it next
to return you to your world.*

Picture death as a stage.
The stage itself is Light.
Wonderful.
Beautiful.
Home.

You, however, are in the wings. You are
still human and you are moving about in
that darkened area, stumbling over props,
tripping over scenery, bumping into each
other, and frightened that you have
forgotten your lines. There is confusion
and turmoil. But the moment that you
step into the Light, it doesn't matter what
the scuffling was before you got to stage
center. It only matters that you are Home
again. Death is like that.

Let me tell you a story about dying.

You live a lifetime. At the end of it you say to those around your deathbed, "What a long life! Why, I lived ninety whole years. Do you know how much I did?" And then you die.

You wake up and ask, "How long was I gone?" The Being of Light who is with you answers, "We hardly noticed you were gone at all. You just sat down and dozed off for a second and here you are again. What kind of a dream did you have this time?"

12
Yes

Dare to believe
the universe is simple.
A loving YES
is the doorway
to infinite possibility.

You were not meant
to understand your life.
You were meant
to live it.

*Do you choose the crucifixion
or the resurrection?*

*We are not speaking of physical death.
That is of no moment at all. We are
speaking of the willingness to die to who
you have been, to be born to who you are.
Every breath you take relives the
crucifixion and the resurrection. Each
exhalation allows all that has been to die.
With inhalation, you are born again into
this moment of Now. Every moment
offers the promise of God. Where is
paradise? Does it have walls? Is there a
map to find it? Need one walk through
the valleys of torment? Does one have to
die physically? I think not.*

It is history that has designed the valleys of torment. One can be in paradise by simply saying "yes" to this moment. Regardless of what seems to be taking place in the illusion of your surroundings, when you say yes you are in loving truth—you are with your own Beingness—you are in no-time, you have touched eternity. You are, indeed, in paradise. The mind will dismiss this as a fairy tale, but the heart knows it is true.

When you deny your "yes" because there is a shred of "no" left and you want to be absolutely sure that you have swept out all the darkness before you can claim your Light, I urge you not to be such a perfectionist. Darkness leads you into the recognition of Light. Then darkness has served you well.

We hear of the struggle between good and evil as being fought within ourselves. In this context who is Hitler?

Your planet, your universe, is an arena of consciousness that allows for the juxtaposition of many things: darkness and light, good and evil, yes and no. It is all designed to aid you in understanding the power of your own YES, the power of your own love, the power of your own Oneness which you are seeking to recall into the cellular consciousness of your body.

Hitler is a mass-created symbol that allows you all to perceive your greatest fears and the nature of your own inner darkness: your own hate, your own arrogance, your own cruelty, your own disbelief.

Who of you has not, much to your own horror, thought of someone and wished he were dead. Of course, you immediately disavow that you had ever harbored such a notion.

The reality, my dears, is that each one of you holds these thoughts. This does not make you evil. As you become aware of them, it makes you far more saintly than those who believe they must deny such thoughts in order to attain sainthood.

So, to acknowledge such impulses and statements is to recognize that a part of you is not yet awake. That part of you believes that the power of anger is greater than the power of love. Perceiving this, you can gently begin to probe where the illusion rests and transform that illusion into Light, into YES.

I would like to know how to open my heart and what the heaviness around it is all about.

My very dear, the heaviness around your heart is the illusion in which you have wrapped yourself to keep your heart safe. Contradiction? Well, illusion *is* contradiction.

When the small child receives the clear message that he is not welcome as he is, then the wound is wrapped in forgetting.

The heaviness around your heart was designed by the child to protect himself from ever, ever being wounded again. But such wrapping shuts out the light and mutes the voice of the heart.

You are longing to be unwrapped, to be free, and the heaviness is the whispered caution that tells you, "It's dangerous."

Close your eyes and welcome the heaviness. It will lighten. In so doing, you bring your self-love into an area that believes it will never be seen, never be heard, never be allowed.

So walk with your heaviness, saying "yes."
Yes to the sadness.
Yes to the whispered longing
Yes to the fear.
YES.

13
The Many Aspects of Self

Self

*You need not remember
the details of yesterday,
last week, last month,
or whose birthday it is.*

*What is essential
is that you remember who you really are.
That is only possible
through your daily,
minute-by-minute, choices.*

As a soul you chose an infant environment that presented you with various models—molds, if you will—into which to pour your divinity. As you choose which ones to activate in this particular life, your karmic workshop is created.

The self was taught that definitions of being good, being worthy, noble, and honorable all had to be sifted through the opinion of another. This is not a criticism of parenting. It is simply the way it is, and it serves a purpose.

At each moment throughout your day, such choices are made. They go something like this: "Who shall I be right now? The one my mother wants me to be? The one my father wants me to be? The one my brothers and sisters hope I'm not? The one my lover thinks I am? The one my children demand I be? Who shall I be?"

Because this practice of choosing is so automatic,
it seldom even ruffles the edges of your active
consciousness. And so you formulate yourselves
in tiny but continuous acts of self-crucifixion,
shaping yourselves to who you believe you are
required to be. You need to become aware
of this habit.

You live your lives within the models you were
given, until a moment arises when you realize
that for all your goodwill and excellent
behavior, you are empty. You touch a longing
that nothing in your world can answer. You
hear a voice calling you to something totally
unfamiliar, *"Be who you are."*

From that moment on, you begin to unravel the tapestry of your life. You may be afraid that you will leave great holes as you pull out threads or change colors or even the theme. Be not afraid. This tapestry is woven of pure illusion.

You are removing the disguises you have wrapped around yourselves in the hope of conforming to what you were taught was "a very good person." *Good for whom and good for what?* You are shrouded in the illusion that you must *do* something, that you must *become* something, that you must *perform* something in order to be worthy.

I see you from my vantage point as angels of Light wrapped in your own self-judgment, bemoaning the lack of freedom that you have denied yourselves.

Just above the mind's tyranny, you would look at one another and ask, "What are we doing? Why do we struggle so? Where are we going?" The times of futility, depression, emptiness in your lives are not because you are unworthy or because life is empty, but because you are following something that does not belong to you, that can never fill you regardless of how perfectly you obey.

All acts that are not perfect love
are acts of self-denial.
Therein lies their pain.

You came again into this world
trailing Light behind you,
harboring the greater Truth.
You may believe
that you have been distracted irrevocably.
Or you may discover that all your life
you have been following that Light.

Whatever your awareness at this point,
there is no mistaking the fact.
You have come as Light,
to transform darkness,
to move ultimately
into the brighter remembering
of the Oneness that you are.

Self and Other

Although the title of this section
is "Self and Other,"
the only real theme
that exists in your human world
is "self and Self."

I want to remind you
of the day you were born.
You decided, as spirit, to enter physicality
and, having done so,
you walked into separation.

It was a courageous act.
As you became physical
you became separated
and everyone else became "other."

Now let us go back to the moment before your birth, back to the essence of Self. This essence knows no fear and no separation. It knows only that it is one with Love.

Remember the experience of finally aligning yourself with physicality. It was that moment when you realized that you were frightened of somebody else, when you pulled back your trusting hands, veiled your adoring eyes, and put the lock and key on your heart.

Don't expect to remember it completely. It was much too painful. It was the worst shock you will ever have in your life.

How can you clearly see others at all, when you see them through such a film of distortion? The first time you recognized other, that other was the agent of separation. They had, by their very existence, crashed through your remembering and taken away your God.

So, what about these others with whom you share your life? Regardless of how estranged or how intimate the relationship may be, you can utilize the otherness only just so far. Then you must step back into Self.

Don't you know that each one of you has the
deepest longing to love everyone? To trust
everyone? To be absolutely vulnerable? Yet you
permit yourselves to be burdened by the oughts
and the ought-not-to's you have taken on.

Just a breath beneath a judgment of a stranger,
there is love and a very dear friend. "Why, I
haven't seen him in three lifetimes!"

Then comes the caution.
"Wait! I can't go walking down the street
loving everybody."

Why can't you? I didn't say you must invade
their privacy with hugs and kisses. Just be
aware of your loving. Do THAT and watch the
change. See faces light up. Notice your cities
becoming safe. Feel the kindness of your world.
You need not say or do a thing. The power of
your love will transform every corner.

Self and World

Before the world existed, you did.
Before anything was manifested
in any of the galaxies,
in any of the recorded universes
you were there.

And I dare say,
after the completion
of this particular round of events,
the entire universe
will dissolve again into Light
and you will be there.

There is nothing strange
about this pronouncement
except for the fact
that most of you don't believe it.

Long before the planets were created, there was
the Oneness of all. In that Oneness was
continual and eternal creation in the name of
love. Elements of You at the cutting edge of
creation said, "In the name of love I will create."
When those portions of You became so involved
in the act of filling the void, you forgot who you
are. There were—and still are—fragments of you
that experience being lost in that void. You have
become the created, rather than remembering
that You are the creator.

Your planet was formed with love to honor the
forgetting of who you are, so that love might
experience itself where love seems not to be.
The pain in your world is the voice of forgetting.

No one can deny the fact that your physical
world is, at this point in time, in a rather
distressful state. Some things are painful.

I am here to remind you that this is not your
primary home. Even as you walk your streets
and read your newspapers and turn the dials
on your television sets and radios, you also
exist here in the world of spirit. The part of you
that treads your earth is quite right in assuming
the world is real. But beyond that, my dears, it
exists only as a vision in your hearts. Notice I
did not say in your minds—but in your hearts.

The heart is the creator, not the mind. Before you physically manifested this world, you envisioned it. In that vision you let love lead, and here you are.

Now what is to be done about the circumstances that exist in your world? What is to be done with the horror, the pain, the starvation, the fear, the grief? If love formulated this planet, how can love now heal it?

The process never stops. Once you begin the act of creation (your beginning in time beyond time), there is no way you can relinquish responsibility for it. You can forget for a while. You can pretend that somehow you are not empowered to reach across the seas to give comfort to a starving child. Yet the truth is you are.

The moment you recognize the infinite power you possess, you will embrace it all again with love and reconnect with the act of creation that originally brought your world into being.

Remember it is You
who have envisioned this wonderful planet
and all the stars and moons
that stretch out seemingly to infinity.

Remember it is you who have come here
to explore your own forgetting,
to reactivate the power of love,
to heal your world
and set it spinning its lovely music
through the rest of its timeless service
until it, too, returns to Light.

Self and God

The act of naming something, though that may
bring it into sharper focus, also tends to separate
it. A label bestows the aspect of "other."

We are discussing Self and God, the very
phasing of which implies separation. There you
have it, my dears, the difficulties of human and
spirit communication. You accept duality with
remarkable ease, and I see it as nonexistent. As
I speak of Oneness, I realize that as the word
enters your brain it becomes fragmented. After
all, the process of becoming human is a
process of fragmentation.

There is a filtering that takes place that belies
the reality of Oneness in your world or you
would not have your world at all. It is difficult
to ascertain with precision where Oneness
becomes fragmented and then, through the
process of human evolution, where
fragmentation begins to blend once more into
Oneness. Your curriculum is only this: "How
Can I Identify Self?" By whatever means you
choose, the task is to recognize and absorb
self into Self with love.

Of course, all things in your universe are God. Does that really mean anything to you: the moment you open your eyes, you recognize distance between you and whoever and whatever else happens to be visible through your physical senses? It is essential for you to believe in the reality of those senses or you would be labeled mad, locked away in some tiresome, musty place and given no credence at all.

You must make one sacred place within you, an inner sanctuary. You must cherish it as your lifeline to Eternal Truth. Forbid the intrusion of the intellect. The higher wisdom is that your Self is the bridge to the Greater Reality. Do not allow physical limitation to encroach upon this holy place which is your connection with Home.

You all know how painful it is when you have found that sanctuary and you then betray it to the tyranny of your human perceptions. Wherever you feel there is a separation between you and the absolute knowing of eternal bliss, you have found a distortion. Wherever there is a sense of fragmentation or wherever you believe you are confined and limited to your physical reality, to your human imperfection, you have found a place of forgetting.

Why do I speak of this? To remove the barrier between self and God. Once that is done, even for a moment, you will recognize the truth of God within you. Then, though you may still stumble over the illusions of separation and limitation, the requirements of your culture, you will never again be captured by them.

You will have come to that perfect moment
when you love yourself perfectly.

You will recognize
the universe you have created.

You will remember
that you are God.

Until that time,
walk sweetly with yourself.
Find every reason possible
to love who you are.

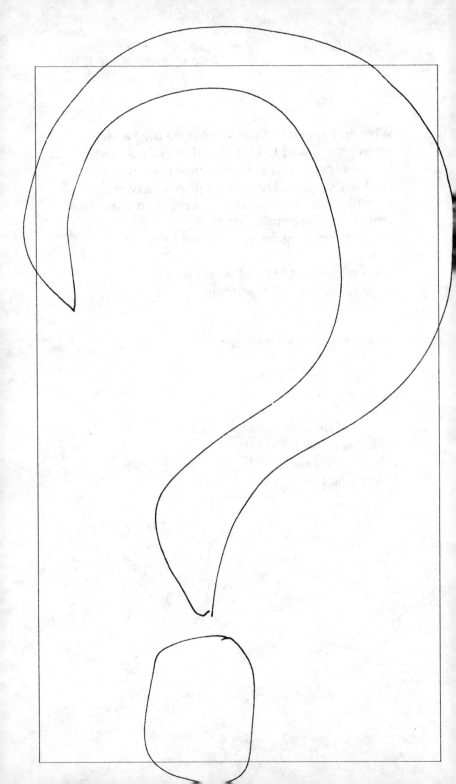

14
Between Our Worlds

Who are you, Emmanuel, and why?

You know who I am.
I am the voice of your remembering.
I am You, beyond the physical costuming,
beyond the walls of forgetting,
beyond the illusion of darkness.

I take no other form.
I claim no other identity.
I use my name because names
are essential in your world.
Would you have come to hear me
if I had said, "I am you?"

There is nothing I know
that you do not.
My task is not to give you
information that is new and different.
My task is to help you remember
what you have forgotten.

And why do I exist?
I like the "why."
I exist by the very miracle of love.
We ARE.
There is no other why.

Is it true that the world of spirit has moved closer?

The world of spirit knows no time or space. Is it more available? It would seem so. Is it because spirit cares more? Not at all.
Perfect Love can only be perfect love.

Many of you are aware of the abundance of guidance that seems to be coming through from the world of spirit. Give it no more value than if it were said to you by someone in physical form. Truth is truth.

In your capacity as seeker, you are also the truth you seek. Should Divine guidance come, even with the rending of the heavens and with trumpets, if it does not feel to *you*, "This is truth," set it aside. The moment you yield rather than stand in your belief, you have dismissed your Self.

At any moment truth can enter.

Whether it be spirit,
a human being,
the laugh of a child,
or the song of a bird,
there will be something
that awakens in you the memory
of who you are.

That is why we all come,
birds, flowers,
dolphins, children,
animals, and you.

Are there indications common to us all that a nonphysical presence is nearby?

There is always a sense of presence:
a warmth,
a feeling of being loved,
a sense of safety.
Often there is a gentle touch,
then a remembering.

You all know the beings
who have been with you
since time began.
They accompany you
to the doorway of birth
and they greet you
at the doorway of your dying.

No act of courage
no act of faith
ever goes unwitnessed.
You are not mysteries
to anyone but yourselves.

You spend your lives
seeking for these loved ones
in the faces of your world.

Emmanuel, did you create yourself?

Oh dear, yes, and so did you. So did we all. In
the beginning, there was no beginning,
and you and I were there.

Let me offer myself as a benign teacher. My
value to you is entirely dependent on how you
would use my presence. I take no sides—
because "right" and "wrong" are not absolutes.
In the Greater Reality, there is only experience.
Since I am here as a representative of the world
of spirit, what then is your relationship to me?
How do you relate to a world you cannot see,
yet all of you without exception know exists?
Oh, some of you say, "I'm only curious." No
you aren't. There is something in each of you
that says, "There *has* to be more to this world."

You are right. There does, and there is.

15
Tools of Remembering: Forgotten Alchemy

The curiosities that you hold about your planet, the mysteries, the frozen and hidden empowerments, are all useful tools for your self-remembering. Once the attention of the student is obtained, the rest is easy. Curiosity is the doorway that stimulates growth, joy, and expansion and allows you to begin to remember who you are.

For the rest of your lives on this planet allow
one minute out of every hour for the
unanticipated. Let yourselves out of prison to
look at your world with unexpecting eyes—eyes
that are not formulated to structure. Reclaim the
wonder of the very small child. Fatigue will go.
Creativity will return. Your heart will open.
Illness will decrease and vanish. Your world
will change.

At any moment you, who are God,
can move mountains
can stop the flow of rivers
can usher in the millennium.

Do the stars ever end and does space ever stop?

From your viewpoint, yes. There is an end to space.
It is at the end of the strongest telescope.
It is also just at the edge
of the farthest stretch of your imagination
where all things end.

From the viewpoint of spirit
the stars do not exist at all.
Nothing exists but lighted essence
swirling around, offering itself to itself
in the name of Love.

This essence
is all that you require
to create a million universes.

See beyond knowing
and you will again touch your infinite power.
Feel beyond knowing in the name of Love
and you will all come Home.

**Could you describe other constellations we don't know
about yet, or have lost or forgotten?**

There is nothing you have lost. I cannot tell you
about other constellations because you have yet
to create them. It is entirely up to you how you
want to fill your heavens.

**Is there an electromagnetic grid which surrounds planet
Earth? Is this grid undergoing changes in its polarity?
Does this kind of movement result in geophysical change
which might be termed cataclysmic?**

Consciousness, of course, can create magnetic
fields. It has, it does, and it will—as one discernible
piece in a network of protective creation.

Is this what science has predicted as calamitous
change? Perhaps. One understands that a
seismograph has no powers of evaluation. It
registers movement and intensity, not cause and
effect. This does not mean that you will watch
devastation and smile. It means that you
will watch, and with your smile, there
will be no devastation.

In your creating (which is your identity, not just
your actions), you have surrounded this
particular planet with the magnetic field of
consciousness that would nurture it, embrace
it, and keep it on course. You can also alter it if
necessary. You will ultimately dissolve your
planet back into Light, which, in truth, it never left.

Please speak to us about the colonization of Earth. Will our completed reincarnational cycles find us in that place of unlimited consciousness? Must we then stay there? Or are we free to experiment with other ways of being?

You are free.
You are free.
You are free.

It will please you to know that there is a part of everyone that dances beyond illusion at all times. You are a bridge from this physical plane to the world of Light and Love.

You came here as Light when consciousness agreed it would be a wondrous thing to create a plane in which to experience what it was like to move in denser matter. Human history sees it as a long, long time. But remember, you have created the illusion of time and of space. This is part of the density. From the greater reality of who you are, this has been only a moment.

Colonized? That word is deceptive. It brings to mind a deliberate movement from one planet to another. I would suggest there has been a frolic from one realm of consciousness to another.

What came first, the chicken or the egg?

Neither. They were created at the same time. At
the moment of creation, there is no linear
concept. In the Eternal Now, there is only the
moment of creation. There, I hope I have finally
answered that question.

**I've heard you say some human beings come from a
star and I've heard some come from other planets.
What does this mean?**

It means your schoolroom is far more expanded
than you thought. The choice is open to
experience life in other areas of the universe.

Are there beings from other planets among us? What are they like? How are they different from us?

Let me remind you that any such guests on your planet are not alien. They are very much a part of you as well. The difference is in memory, not in essence.

You are not the only consciousnesses spinning around in this illusion. When you are willing to accept that there are others on other planets, you allow for their creation. Can you hear in that the compassion for self? Humanity now requires companions. You no longer want to live in isolation as the only ones in the vastness, so you have allowed for neighborhood.

Are your neighbors like you? They are about as similar as your neighbors next door, which is to say much the same yet very different.

Do they have similar molecular structure? Yes. They may have different density, but they are created from the same stuff of consciousness that you are. There is nothing else. Every tree, each blade of grass is who you are.

Each form of life from miniscule to vast is love forming itself around its own needs, its own truth, its own reality. If you will look up into the nighttime sky you will see what a splendid job you have done. There *you* are, spinning around, twinkling, moving through space. As the microscopic world becomes more available, you will look inside and there *you* are again, the same consciousness doing the same dance.

Move beyond
who you think you are.
Stretch beyond
who you believe you ought to be.
We must leap among the stars
you and I together.

How many times is it necessary to return to the physical classroom?

It depends entirely on your willingness to awaken. If you do so with alacrity, why, you will whiz through in perhaps three or four centuries. Some of you may take a little longer.

Where do souls stay between incarnations?

There is no halfway house. The moment you
are out of your body, you are Home.

What can you tell us of parallel and alternative lives?
Would it help us now to know more about them?

One cannot heal fragmentation by walking
through fragmentation.

In the Oneness, fragmentation ceases to be.
The illusion of chronological time and space
dissolves and all you would attempt to
understand through the reckoning of parallel
lives becomes evident. All lives, whether lived
simultaneously or chronologically, are designed
for one purpose: to bring the light of
remembering into the area of darkness.

Science tells us our bodies are porous. In the spaces
between the cells of our bodies another shape is defined
in reverse. Is this second outlined space part of us,
another form of matter, another entity?

Another level of consciousness.

Could you define the aura?

*Your aura
is the energy source
that is you
attempting to fit itself
into a physical body.*

*Because it is so vast
it spills over.
You walk in a glow
of Greater Self.*

Are tears of joy and tears of sorrow the same?

The tears of grief are the easing of pain. Tears of
joy have a different chemical component than
those of grief. Why would this not be so? In joy,
one needs to burst from the confines of
nonexpression, and tears are the spilling forth
into the universe.

How may we talk to the devas and angels and how is my grandmother doing?

That is an appropriate question, just as it's worded.

How may you talk to them? Next time you take a walk in the woods, allow your peripheral vision to be active. Be willing to see out of the corner of your eye and you will observe marvelous things.

Having perceived them, you must do them honor and ask for permission to speak. They are very shy, for they have been relegated to the realm of fantasy for so long that some have quite begun to believe it themselves.

Give them the benefit of the doubt. Acknowledge their reality. They will be grateful to you and they will serve you, but only in the name of love.

How is your grandmother? Delighted. The words she wants me to speak are:

"Listen. Just listen.
Hear the voice of the wind
of the trees
and of your own heart
and somehow, in some way,
I will speak to you through that."

What are the magical properties of toning and chanting?

It is a remarkable practice that allows you to bring into physicality the higher vibrations that stimulate transformation. The vibrational experience allows the density to tremble a bit so that it can begin to slough off some of the heaviness. Rather like dusting yourselves.

Everything has a vibratory essence and carries its unique tone. Even the movement of blood in your veins emits its own sound. *You* are music.

Ask yourselves, "What does love sound like?" and then make that sound. The desire to be in harmony is, in itself, a statement of love.

Expand beyond thought, and you will find the capacity to experience sound remarkably enhanced. There is a symphony constantly playing in your lives.

Sound
is the music of creation
creating itself.

What can you tell us about our dreams?

There are three major categories of dreaming,
and each one has individual variations
within each theme.

There are dreams in which you barely lift from
your physical world. You float about, perhaps
on the ceiling of your bedroom, mulling over
the day's activities, translating them into
vocabularies that will reveal as well as conceal
what it is you are afraid to know (yet already do).

Then there are the nights when you leave your
bodies and work in your world where love calls
you. You seem to be resting in your bed, but
you are, in truth, flying about your planet being
angels of mercy. These often are dreams you do
not remember upon awakening but, in time,
you will begin to recall having been in places of
healing, at accidents, having taken the hand of a
lost child, or rescuing a dog. Wherever you are
needed in the name of love, you will be there.
Look at the wonderful work you have been doing
when you thought you were just lying asleep!

Does this sound fanciful? It is not. Remember those mornings when you had thought you had gone to bed early enough and you wonder why you are tired. It is because you have been out doing good works. Take pleasure in that.

The greatest dreaming is when you leave your bodies completely and come Home. As you awaken in the morning, you are refreshed. You know full well you have been somewhere wonderful and you have been touched with Perfect Love.

Why do I feel so close to dolphins?

Dolphins are saying to the world, "This is my way to manifest love. Show me yours." Dolphins swim in a wondrous light of joy, of selfless, loving wonder. Who would not be drawn to them?

But they are not the only creatures of light and joy and wonder. You are too.

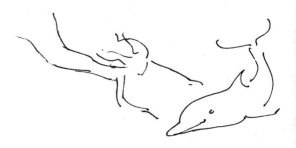

What sort of evolutionary path does the mineral kingdom follow? How does it interact with the human kingdom?

The mineral kingdom is not so much in need of evolution as you might suppose. All things on your planet are not locked in forgetting. The mineral kingdom knows it is here to represent its own vocabulary of eternal truth.

Those of you who are exploring the world of crystals are being reminded of a greater truth through this particular form of consciousness. You are recognizing that within what seems to be solid matter, the voices of angels sing. Indeed, a blade of grass, a feather from a bird's wing, and, as the poet writes, a grain of sand holds All-That-Is. Each thing in its seeming separation is created from the Whole, from the Oneness, and so are you.

You are the students
on your planet.
Rocks do not need to study.
They are here to teach.
Trees have nothing to learn.

Let the world speak to you.
When was the last time
you sat with a butterfly?

Are there any new science–spirit breakthroughs coming soon?

Science is discovering that there are things that go beyond itself. You will utilize science to prove to yourselves that love is all there is.

It is wondrous to see illusion follow itself to its own enlightenment.

What is true alchemy?

True alchemy is the transformation of the energy of fear into the power of love.

Who says
two and two are four?
Think about it.
Just because it's in physically manifested
apples and pears?

I would like to play
a delightful game.
Throw it all up in the air
and ask yourself
"Two?"

What, indeed, does "two" mean?
If all things are ONE
the whole illusion of two
is nonsense.

So two and two make One,
don't they?
And four and four make One
and six and six make One.

There.
You've just reclaimed your brain.

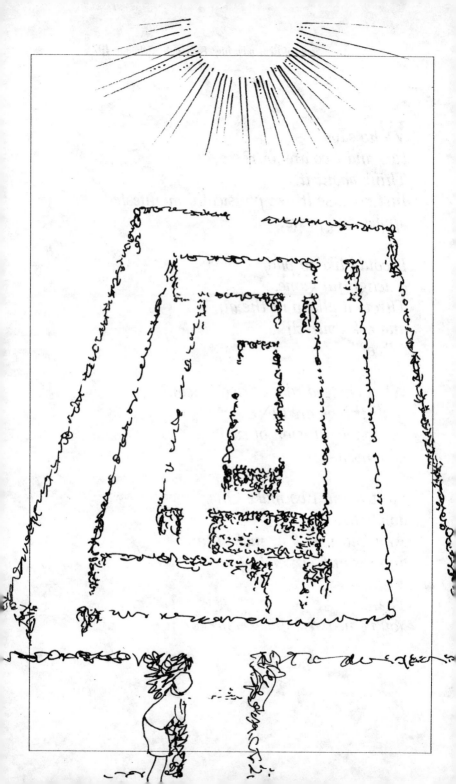

16
Any Path
Will Bring You Home

Your world of illusion is too fond of drawing
maps. When something calls you, follow it. Do
not be afraid. The only path you are really on is
your own. It is all illusion anyway. *In the Greater
Reality you have never been on any path, because
you have never left Home.*

Is everything really occurring at its perfect time? If so, what is the role of effort?

Loving effort honors your own commitment. Yet truth was not meant to be the boulder pushed up the mountain.

Fear dotes on effort. It says, with great pride, "There, wasn't that hard? If it isn't difficult, it has no value." Fear is trying to make love feel guilty. One gets medals for strenuous effort. No one has ever been given an award for sitting in bliss.

Is the clock of salvation on time?
Yes. But let me tell you something
about salvation's time:
it's Now.

Beyond Now is only fear
and fear keeps a great many clocks.

How can I achieve enlightenment?

Enlightenment
is you
undefined by fear.

Do I mean
you are already enlightened?
Indeed I do.
You have only forgotten.

Forgetting is not the truth,
remembering is.
You will lose nothing of value
when you choose to remember,
when you choose love.

All you will lose
is history.
Have you any idea
how heavy history is?

What of spiritual teachers who insist on rigid disciplines? The practices you "must do every day"? I have such love and respect for these teachers, yet there is a dichotomy between the love and the demand.

Your question is not as important as fear would make it. One who would say, "You must walk my way," is, at some time in your life, a savior and, at another time, a tyrant. Each teacher is a hand to hold to help you over some difficult terrain. There is no one teaching guaranteed to bring you to heaven. Indeed, the truth of the matter is that you have never left heaven.

You are all seekers and knowers of truth. You will not make a wrong turn because the purpose of your life is to move through your human personality and ultimately find the courage to remember who you are. If a strident teaching takes you from a room of fear into a room of knowing, does the nature of the teaching make a difference? Is it not important only that you are here? Do not demand that your histories paint a picture that will convince you of the validity of your own spiritual wisdom. This does not make a mockery of your life. It makes it a safe adventure.

I am not saying
that it does not matter what you do.
I am saying
that what you do matters so much
that the labels and details of it
do not matter.

I start out being disciplined in my spiritual practices, then I fall back and stop. I feel I have let the cosmos down.

Self-indulgence is not the way to clarity, but neither is self-discipline in the manner that denies your selfhood. Find something that you *do* want to do. There is no purpose for discipline other than to quiet the mind, and if the mind is in rebellion, it will not be quieted.

The only thing required on the spiritual path is your commitment to truth, your longing to find love of self and love of God. This one commitment will bring you Home regardless of how many careless things you do, regardless of how many days you allow yourself to be happy. Be clear with that commitment and leave the rest to your own good wisdom.

How do we access our own inner voice?

Learn, in your solitude, the way to your inner sanctuary. You will eventually wear a path there.

To get to the silence, you must go through what might appear to be a mined field. There are so many denials, objections, what if's. The way to that sanctuary can indeed sound like the Fourth of July. How, then, does one get there? One first must be willing to listen to the fireworks. It will be educational. You have no idea how filled with noise you are. The illusion that seems to demand your constant attention is insatiable. Only in your silence can the Greater Reality touch you. Only in your silence can it be received.

If the karmic path is set out for us, how does the power of prayer intervene?

Prayer is God speaking to Itself. Prayer is talking to Yourself and listening to Yourself on the many levels of greatness that You, in your humanness, have forgotten.

Prayer is the voice that moves beyond the intellect. It has infinite power to move you to the heart of your being and so dissolve the structures that cause you pain.

Are there conscious dark or evil forces at work in opposition to God?

No. No. No. There is only ignorance, which breeds fear. Fear creates what seems to be darkness. When you consider that all things are God, how could there be evil?

Revelation walks in Light. One's eyes must become accustomed to the brilliance before one can see God. Walk in the dappled light of your human experience, denying neither the shadow nor the light, but embracing *all*. Your task as a human being is to bridge the worlds.

You have no way of knowing from what direction God will next become apparent.

Is organized religion a spiritual path?

Organized religion is a memory of known truth. Yet formalizing anything takes it out of the moment of its purity.

Anything that tells you, "This path is the only way Home," is teaching fear. Religion's initial intent was to honor loving truth, but in its anxiety that truth cannot exist without structure, it has all but destroyed what it originally attempted to honor.

Are monastic periods necessary for spiritual growth?

Only if you think they are.

In meditation it's all so simple. Why does everything get so complex when I open my eyes?

Because you have been taught to believe what your eyes see rather than what your inner eye knows. A switch of allegiance is needed.

Can we trust our own mental perceptions?

Mental perception uses the vocabulary of
finiteness, of limitation, of fear, to describe
fearlessness. The intellect can recognize truth
but it can never explain it.

You have a truth detector inside you
which is absolutely accurate.
Some of you call it hindsight.
That is only because you didn't listen
when it spoke the first time.

**All spiritual paths counsel forgiving and releasing self
and others so that we can be in the present. Can you give
me some *practical* advice on how I can really release
resentment?**

The first practical thing I can say to you is that
holding on to anger, fear, resentment, and all
the stuff of which fear is made is the most
impractical thing you can do. It robs your energy.
It burdens your heart and makes your body ill.
It causes you to despair so that you do not see
the sunrise or hear the song of a bird. It interferes
with your happiness and takes up entirely too
much room in your thoughts. Therefore,
something must be done. You are right.

When spiritual paths hold the commandment
that you forgive those who have harmed you,
you are already heavy-laden with extra guilt. At
the moment of hearing that injunction, you
have absolutely no intention of letting those
who have wounded you off the hook.

Rather than berate yourself for holding negative
feelings, let us take a more practical approach.
Examine each resentment to find its core of
truth. What was going on inside you as you
chose resentment or unforgiveness? You always
have a choice to love or fear. Resentment is a
form of fear.

Now move into the present as though you were
a brand-new tribunal, which of course you are.
With your next breath, your angry response
from the past is totally irrelevant. When I speak
of living in the Now, when I speak of releasing
yourself from history, I am offering you just this
choice with every breath you take. You carry
around great knapsacks of irrelevancy and you
wonder why you are tired!

Is perfect enlightenment possible for us on this earth?

The moment you stop being afraid, you are perfectly enlightened. The course of action is up to you.

Is perfect anything possible in your world? Yes, a thousand times yes. But your vocabulary of "perfect" will not be satisfied. You have images of perfection predicated upon what fear thinks it ought to be. Are you willing to release them?

Stand without fear and you are perfect. Will you still be imperfect in your human personality? Oh, perhaps others would say so, but it won't bother you a bit. *That* is enlightenment.

How will I know the voice of God?

You each receive that voice in your own vocabulary, your own experience. God speaks to each one individually. This contact is so individual that there is not another person on the planet who can describe for you what it will be.

All expectation
must be put aside
until the recognition
that God is everything
is accepted by the inner being.

Then the voice of God
is heard everywhere.

When you learn to love,
to trust, to believe in yourself,
you know God as the center
of who you are.

How can I know God's Will?

When you begin to unravel those layers of fear that have given you a sense of safety and identity in your world, you will find that you and God are one. You will know God's will then, for it will be your own.

17
Out of History
into the NOW

Let me give you a lesson in NOWness.

You race from here to there, denying yourself
the fulfillment of the NOW. This moment, the
NOW, this eternal "hereness" is what
constitutes your life.

When you remain in the present, the future offers
a wide variety of ways and means by which to
serve you. If you ask for an answer and focus in
one direction only, assiduously denying all
other possibilities in the name of historic
consistency, you receive but a shadow of what
is available.

In reality, you have no way of knowing what
the next instant will bring regardless of how
carefully you have planned. There is nothing
for you to do but experience what is here.
Living in the moment sets you free.

Don't you have to plan some things?

There is a subtle difference between making
reasonable arrangements and becoming locked
into them. To be trapped in future projection or
limited by your history does not serve you.
Who you are is not who you were is not who
you will be.

Isn't that frightening?

In the NOW, fear does not exist. You could walk
through the doorway of death in absolute
peace. You could move through what observers
might describe as a horrifying experience, yet in
your centeredness you would know no fear. You
would only know Self. When fear enters, it is
because you have moved back into history or
projected into the future from one illusion
to another.

In the NOW will we have painful feelings?

No. When you allow yourself your absolute
beingness, there is no need for pain, fear, or
any of those voices in your human world that
serve to remind you that you are not in the NOW.

So we would no longer cry?

Perhaps you will weep, but not for yourselves.
No tears of sadness. You relinquish history
when you say "yes" to the moment. Sorrow
lives only in the past.

**Can you tell us about the evolutionary stages of this
practice of living in the *NOW*?**

If I did you would place it in structure.

Evolution has as its goal the concept of no
evolution. You speak from within time and
space. Beyond time and space, there is only
beingness.

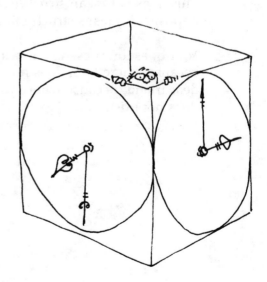

You talk of "going Home." If there is no time or space, are we actually going somewhere?

Let me offer you an opportunity to examine where you are at this moment in the light of infinite possibility and unmanifested potential. When referring to potential, we must be cautious. Potential to you denotes past, present, and future. To me, it means the Eternal NOW in its infinite unfoldment as NOW moves from NOW to NOW.

In the beginning of creation that has ever been and will ever be, all things were allowed to come into form. I refer not only to physically manifested matter. I speak of form of possibility. This does not mean structure. Quite the opposite. It means structureless potential.

Your question presents me with difficulty, not because where I am does not exist but rather, dear friend, because where you are does not exist.

Is reincarnation true? I'm not sure I believe in it.

Oh, yes, and it doesn't demand that you believe
in it. Within illusion, belief systems are
important. Outside of illusion, they have no
relevance. You affect the universe not at all by
your failure to believe in it. You do, however,
affect your own life by your beliefs.

How does reincarnation work if there's no time?

Consciousness, in eternal NOWness, evolves.
You see reincarnational sequences as
progression: as past, present, and future.
Beyond time, You create yourselves constantly
from the experiences You invite within time.

**If we let go of all our history, wouldn't we be like the
child who thinks only of his momentary comforts with
no consideration for others?**

The harvest of your history frees you. With
such unbound freedom, your capacity to love is
the light that not only illuminates your way but
assists others as well.

If you are seduced by the siren song of history,
you deny the purpose for which that history
has been designed, which is to bring you to this
point in time.

NOW is eternity which has chosen to take
physical form.

Walking your earth or eating a meal or seeing
the trees change or hearing a bird—none of
these exist until you touch them.

I hear your minds. "Emmanuel, are you telling
me that until *I* experience a tree, it doesn't
exist?" I am. And am I telling you that until you
hear the song of a bird, that bird is not singing?
Not the way you hear it. Everything in your world
is neutral until you touch it. Is that not magic?

What does one do with such information? You
enjoy it, and know that the particular birdsong
you hear has never been heard before. You are
so important in your world that, without you,
what you touch with your presence would
literally not exist.

Then is our history all a lie?

Not while it is happening. In retrospect,
absolutely. One cannot view the NOW
faithfully from any historical perspective.

There is not one of you who does not walk in
the colorless atmosphere of memory, when
your hearts are longing to be in the Light of
NOW, to celebrate your life. You feel burdened
because you remember burdens. When you are
laughing, if your mind is still, the entire
universe laughs.

The message from the world of spirit can be
stated with simplicity:

Perfect love is all there is
and perfect love must be experienced
in the NOW.
All else
is fear's complexity.

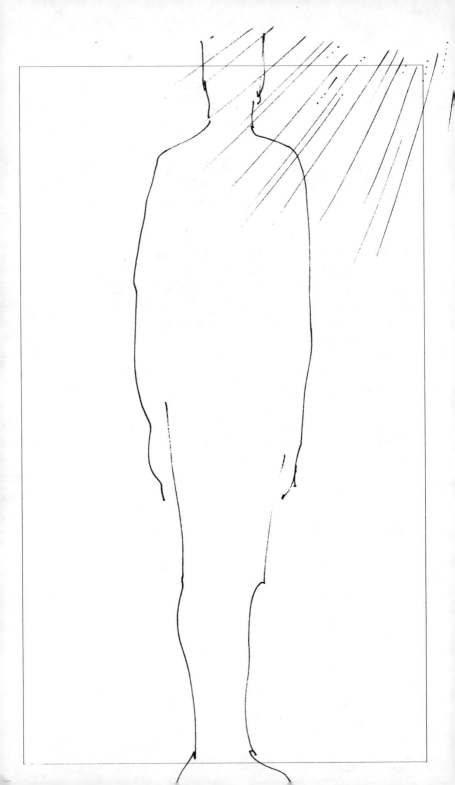

18
The I AM

The creator, the perceiver,
knows I AM.
The perceived, the created
is fraught with I am not.

The Beingness of you
is the center of the universe,
is All-That-Is:
all-powerful,
all-loving,
all-perfection,
all Light.

Even as you are the created,
you are the creator.
Even as you are the perceived,
you are the perceiver.

To blend the I AM and the I am not
you have called yourselves
into this world again
and again and again.

You find opportunities,
throughout your lives,
to come to a point of equilibrium
where you know that you are both
spirit and human,
mind and heart,
love and fear,
One and separate.

In these moments of supreme recognition,
love sighs, "At last,
I have come Home."

At these same moments,
there is an exquisite excitement
as fear says, "Now I have found the key!
I must quickly write it down,
label and file it
lest it escape me."

At that moment
it is lost.

What is to be done?

It is not so difficult, loved ones.
Just be willing
to offer yourselves your lives.

Remind yourselves,
"This moment belongs to me.
My history may have belonged to others
and my future I have yet to create.

This moment is mine.
It is the only thing that exists
in the universe.
All else is illusion.
All else is dream."

With that insight,
you will be at that pivotal point
of truth
where you are both perceived
and perceiver.

Why the separation of physical and spiritual, since we are all one?

You have merely entered the illusion of separation. It is as if you have all undertaken to put on a play. You choose parts and you agree, as you walk onto the stage, that that which you know to be unreal is real for the duration of the drama. You live as though you believe your own performance—a play within a play.

There are infinite ways that Love can create itself in the name of Itself. *One* of the ways is to become human—to see what love is like, what it does, and where its power lies in the theater where love has been separated from Itself.

For this you have manifested a world where you can live in the illusion of fragmentation. This is a wondrous way to experience Self—in this nation, that climate, this body, that religion. What is God like in poverty? How is love in pain? What is love's dance with Itself?

You return to Oneness with a greater gift of awareness than when you reached out in your Godhood to create this world.

You are not here on a useless errand to suffer at the whim of a greater power. You are here for a beautiful purpose: to know the loving I AM within the circumstances of your life.

It is a lovely journey
for it is the journey of love.
You move from the center of All-That-Is
to expand to the edge of creation
and beyond.

Once in my life I touched the circle from which you radiate. I long for it again.

It is only the shadows of forgetting
that cause you all to believe
that the Light is somewhere else.
It is within you.

Dear Emmanuel, why do we forget?

Picture this, a center of Light. That is who you are. That is all there is. As Light expands to fill the void, as you expand to fill emptiness with Self, the edge of you that is creating the yet-to-be-created stands at the next moment of eternity.

In that moment there is confusion. Those portions of you that are at the cutting edge of creation have already forgotten in order to identify with what is to be rather than with the act of creation itself.

Self-love brings you back into alignment. You *remember* and the void is filled with love.

*H*uman definition
is like a child's drawing
upon the sand.
A wave washes in
and with a sigh
all is Oneness again.

I feel as though there are many me's inside. How then do I find the I AM?

The framework upon which the many stand is the I AM-ness before it moves into fragmentation. Embrace the many.

You are whole. You are complete. You ARE. You moved into the illusion of multiplicity because your journey required it. And yet You never left Oneness at all.

Is this white light me? Is this devil me? Is this life's paradox?

Is the white light who you are? Of course, but much more than that. The I AM that animates your body knows itself to be human. It assumed minuteness in order to fit your physical form while still holding the essence of the Greater Self. In your world, there seems to be a refraction of this light into many colors. When you remove yourself from the center of your I AM, you will see all manner of manifestations of the Self: you are rose-colored, you are purple, you are green, you are yellow. You are fragmented. Is the Greater You available? Yes, in your remembering.

Are you devil? Only if you perceive forgetting as evil. Is there duality in your world? Yes, when you remove yourself from the center of the I AM.

The I AM is the treasure that you have kept sacred within you. It is your tenderness and it is your infinite wisdom and power in the name of loving truth. That is your I AM.

Do I look to my I AM every day, or maybe once or twice during meditation? Once I find out who I am, how can I go back to the office?

*Look for who you are
as often as you think of it.*

*Whenever you feel
the slightest discomfort,
dis-ease, lostness, fear,
perplexity, or longing, you know
you have stepped outside
of your I AM.*

*Step back in.
There will come a time
when being inside the I AM
is more familiar
than being outside the I AM.
Perhaps then, my very dear,
you won't go to the office.*

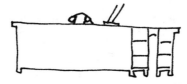

**In Buddhist teachings I learned that there is no big "I."
How do I understand the I AM in relation to this?**

The I AM, as you experience it in your
physicality, is the manifested Buddha. If you
choose to follow your teachings, they will take
you wherever you wish them to.

**What am I going to do when I have reached my
highest form?**

You are not going to *do* anything. You are going
to *be*. And in your creative Beingness, you will
dance through the heavens.

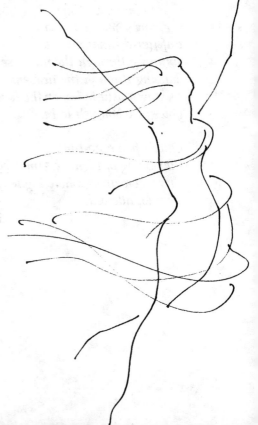

Someone told me a story. Once upon a time, there was a
thought. That thought became a soul. That soul encased
itself in living flesh. The flesh was beaten and abused,
but the thought-soul was never touched.
Why do I not feel worthy?

Once upon a no-time
there was a thought.

The thought
was not the thought of thinking.
The thought was the beingness
of the heart.

Once upon a no-time
there was You
unfettered, unafraid
spinning through the universe
dancing through the heavens
seeking a way to honor the love
you knew Yourself to be.

Once upon a no-time
that Being of Light remembered
there were areas where Light
was not allowed.

That act of remembering
brought you here.

In the language of that story
thought is love
not limited by the intellect's capacity
to understand.

There are moments in your life
when you are absolutely clear
in your remembering.

Your feelings of unworthiness
reflect your denial
of the reality of those moments.
You chose fear.

There is no pain in life
other than self-betrayal.
What else can harm you?

Why are there more and more people on the earth each day? How does this fit in with reincarnation?

When something wonderful is about to happen, consciousness will multiply itself. It will embody itself in triplicate. Am I predicting something wonderful? I do not indulge in predictions, for it is not I who is creating your world. It is you. Yet it does seem, does it not, as though the signs were pointing to wondrous times?

Oh, I know. Some rumors afoot say that the world will be destroyed or humanity will blow itself up. That is nonsense.

You have all come to witness the lifting of the veil, to be present when the remembering of who you are takes place. I will go even further. When humanity finally comes to terms with the futility of fear (and you are moving there swiftly), you will begin to experience great moments of illumination. This is why you have all come. None of you wants to miss the global awakening.

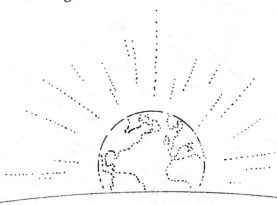

What is needed most on earth?

You.